FITTING IN AND FORGIVEN

_May the _____ A Child of God Psalm 18:16_

Mary Ann Young

outskirts
press

Outskirts Press, Inc.
http://www.outskirtspress.com

ISBN: 978-1-9772-1572-7

Outskirts Press and the "OP" logo are trademarks belonging to Outskirts Press, Inc.

PRINTED IN THE UNITED STATES OF AMERICA

I dedicate this book to my husband.

Tim, thank you for your gentle hand,

words, and prayers that continued to bring

me back to the completion of this book.

I can honestly say you are my biggest cheerleader.

I'm forever grateful to God for you.

I love you forever ...

Because I realize what happens
in a young girl's life now
is life lasting in her heart …

A great woman is

She who has not lost

The heart of a child.
~Mencius~

Jesus, may you open each tender heart to know you ...

Table of Contents

CHAPTER 1

Cliques: Test of True Friendship

Friends, at times I think it's a love-hate relationship. I mean, sometimes we are just so happy hanging out with our friends, laughing with them, and sharing our hearts with them, that it feels like our friends are truly the best thing in our lives. They're contagious you might say, to where we just can't get enough time being with them. But, then, crazy as it is, there are also those times when we are slamming the doors closed on them, hanging the phone up on them, sending them a bad text, or worse we're talking trash about them to others. Oftentimes ending in a fit of anger and wanting revenge. When I think about it our friendships can be like an emotional roller coaster—one minute we are up and happy and the other minute we feel like we are at our all-time lowest, to the point where we may lose the contents of our stomach. And in all honesty, I'm no angel either. And I would be lying if I said that I've never caused pain to one of my friends before, either by something I said or did to them. Would you say that's true of you too? I believe whether intentional or not, we have all hurt some of our friends. And I can truly tell you that it does not ever stop with friendship problems, unfortunately …

What does change is that we learn how to pick better friends and we learn how to become a better friend. In my opinion, one of the best Bible verses to look at when it comes to dealing with our friends is Matthew 7:12, which says,

"Do to others whatever you would like them to do to you."

This truly sounds simple enough to do, but living it out is not that easy at all. Oh, sure, sometimes it's a cinch to be nice to our friends and love them, but other times our selfish nature takes control and we end up expecting our friends to treat us well, while we act as though we don't care anything about them. Sound familiar? I am also thinking of those of you who at this very moment are really upset; your heart is hurting because someone, maybe a friend, has been mean to you. And you're thinking, I didn't do anything wrong, I always treated this person fair and nice but she hates me, and I can't believe what she did to me. I'm so sorry if that's what is going on in your world right now. The truth is, girls can be so cruel. Right? I know this to be true because I'm a girl and I know how mean I can be at times, or have been …

Now do you see what I mean, that if we lived out the truth of Matthew 7:12 and treated others the way we ourselves want to be treated, we'd radically stop the vicious cycle of mean girls??? …

Although I don't know exactly what you are hurting over, I do know how it feels to be lied about, left out, whispered about, and laughed at, told I was ugly and fat, not invited to the party or lunch, not picked for the team. Honestly, I could go on and on … man, it hurts even recalling those times …I know the pain you are feeling is real, and my heart goes out to you with a big supernatural hug, because I know how bad it really does hurt. Sometimes it hurts much more than we will even admit or let others know about. Right? But may I give you a ray of hope? A bit of truth. Even though it does not feel like it right now, this thing you are dealing with will pass. In time, it will get easier on you and one day you might even forget about it. What you are personally going through right now is teaching you; it's actually cementing into your brain how you would <u>never</u> want to treat another person, especially someone you called a friend. It's my hope and prayer for you that you will grow from this hurtful time, and that you will grow for the better with greater understanding in how to be a true friend.

And if you are hurting right now because of a friendship gone wrong, it might help for you to reflect and think about all the facts of what happened to you in this situation. How has it affected you? Are you sad, hurt, angry, fearful, or embarrassed? Now let's think about how it affected the other person or persons involved. I know that it's not an easy thing to do to consider the person or person's feelings who hurt you, but the truth of the matter is they're human too, and well, we all get hurt over the same things. All of us girls can be broken down very easily. Truly, what hurts you, hurts me, and it hurts every girl that we know in very much the same way. So, let's try and put aside your feelings and look at ways you could have handled this situation differently. You see, as girls, most of the time we take everything that happens to us so personally and emotionally, and if we would have just acted differently when something happened, it might not have snowballed so badly out of control.

So, let's look at the facts and see if by your doing something differently (saying something different, thinking differently, not telling anyone, or not giving that look or sending that text) it could have changed the outcome. You can't change what happened now, but you can learn from this situation and stop it from happening again. If only, girls, we could look at things more logically sometimes, and not so emotionally, I really do think it would help us all greatly.

And this may sound strange, but let's invite God into this situation with your friend or friends and ask Him for help in what is going on. Let's ask for Him to show you if you are in the wrong in any way, and let's ask Him to take away any anger that you may have in your heart right now towards them.

Let's do that now:

Dear Lord, You know everything that just happened to me. You even knew it was going to happen long before it did. Would you please help my heart to feel better, to be back to normal, bring peace in this situation, and could you please show me if I am at fault in any way? Amen.

You see, anger in our hearts leads to wrong actions—ones that will cause more harm to us in the long run. Don't let this lead into name calling, because we all know how bad that feels. Name calling really does do a lot of harm; in fact, it truly kills a part of us. We've all heard the little tale that sticks and stones may break our bones, but words will never hurt us. But, it's not true, is it? What a bunch of lies that is! Words do hurt us <u>Big</u>-time! And honestly, we really do heal a lot faster from broken bones than from broken hearts. In fact, I have heard that broken bones can heal back better and stronger than before they were ever broken. But hurtful words spoken to us leave deep-lasting scars ... that never seem to heal. Right?

I think as girls we need to admit:

- that at times our intentions are cruel

- that our own insecurities make us put others down

- that we tease others over their flaws that they can't do much about

"The words you say will either acquit you or condemn you." ~Matthew 12:37

Allow for that scripture to sink in for a minute ...

We are also so sensitive. I believe as girls, we are way more tuned in to how something comes across in a person by the sound of their words, looking at their facial expressions, and their body posture, like the crossing of their arms. And don't bother with the sweet talk when your face and body language are not looking so sweet. That just doesn't work for us—words and actions must line up. Right? We know how to interpret it all ... There's an old Irish proverb that says, "Say it little but say it well." I so agree with that Irish saying!

"The ear tests the words it hears just as the mouth distinguishes between foods." ~Job 12:11 NLT

Think about how sensitive we are:

There is a huge difference in the comparison of our bodies to a little ant's body. Right? Yet, when one little ant starts to crawl on our bodies, say like on our hand, we feel it crawling on us instantly. I believe there is a reason why God made us to be sensitive, both physically and emotionally. And I believe it's our responsibility to use our special sensitivity when it comes to talking to others or talking about others, especially our friends.

President Calvin Coolidge said, "I never have regretted anything I didn't say." Wow! We often regret what we say, but it's simply impossible to regret saying something if we never ever have said it before! President Coolidge was wise to bite his tongue, and we would be wise if we bit our tongues more too.

THINK
T - is it truthful?
H - is it helpful?
I - is it inspiring?
N - is it needful?
K - is it kind?

If what you are talking about has all those things then go ahead and keep talking, but if even one of them is lacking, please be quiet!

Gossip

Gossip is something none of us like, yet every one of us listens to it. I honestly think when we hear gossip about someone else, it makes us feel better about ourselves. Deep down we are grateful and relieved to know that the gossip is not about us. But that's so sad when you think about it, because sooner or later someone will be talking bad about us too. It always seems to happen ...

Did you know that gossip can be a total lie or it can also be the truth? Let's say you got a bad grade on a test score and someone other than you saw it, then that person goes and tells everyone at school that you got an F on that test. Well, it may be true, but it was not something you wanted everyone to know about. So, according to T-H-I-N-K it is true, but it's sure not helpful, or inspiring, needful or kind. Right? No, it's not, and it's called gossip, and gossip hurts the one who is being blabbered about. What we say about others will either lift them up or tear them down. It's horrible to be gossiped about!!! We need to stop doing it! The truth is we all get bothered by the same things. We all hate gossip, so we all need to stop spreading it and stop listening to it. Gossip stinks and it stings! And did you know that gossip starves a friendship but it feeds a crowd? It does because when you pass around gossip about your friend, you are causing distance between you and that friend, maybe to the point of you two not ever being friends again. Yet, all the while you are starving that friendship, you are also attracting a crowd of people listening to you gossip about her. Ears are always up and tuned in when gossip is going around, unfortunately ...

Proverbs 11:13 says, **"A gossip goes around telling secrets, but those who are trustworthy can keep a confidence."**

<u>Girls, let's recycle our trash only and not our conversations!</u>

"You see me when I travel and when I rest at home. You know everything I do. You know what I am go- ing to say even before I say it, Lord."
~Psalms 139:3–4

Girls, God knows every word on our tongues (everything we say), and that means every word we speak is being broadcast straight to heaven. With that knowledge, it should change the way we talk along with every word we say, especially when we are talking about other people.

Friends

Now some of you have a bunch of friends, others of you have only one friend, and some of you may feel as though you don't have any friends. But having several friends has its own problems, because now you're having to deal with many personalities to get along with, and also jealousies, misunderstandings, not to mention several birthdays to buy for. LOL on the birthday presents ...

Proverbs 18:24: **"There are friends who destroy each other, but a real friend sticks closer than a brother."**

I've found it's easier to be a good friend to just one other per- son than trying to be a good friend to several other girls. Because at some time or another we will forget about one of our other friends, and they will feel left out or unimportant. Even though we didn't mean to be a bad friend, we can make someone feel like we are. So, to you who have a lot of friends I say, be careful. To those of you who have one great friend, be thankful. And to those who feel as though they don't have a friend right now, you really do. His name is Jesus and he truly loves everything about you. Sweet girls, those of you with big hearts, why don't you go befriend a girl that you see who seems to be all by herself. By doing so, you just might find out that she'll be the nicest, sweetest friend you've ever had. No one likes to be alone, so be bold and go talk to her. ☺

I think it's wise to not call any of our friends our BFFs. When we give them that title then it seems weird when a friendship changes, and you aren't very close any more to that person. We all go through many friendship changes, and even though we think our friendships won't change, they can, and they do. Something to think about ...

What to look for in a good friend

Think about this with me for a minute: When Moses came down from the mountain after receiving the Ten Commandments his face glowed, because he had been with God (see Exodus 34:29). So, too, do our faces change and start looking more like those we hang out with. It's way better to glow to others than glare at them. So, choose your friends wisely! Because we make choices and then those choices make us ...

"Wounds from a sincere friend are better than many kisses from an enemy." ~Proverbs 27:6 NLT

Does this scripture make any sense to you? Let me share my thoughts on this verse. A true friend at times could do something or say something that hurts you, but their intentions were to help you. Let's say those wounds could be your friend telling you:

- you shouldn't have stolen something

- you shouldn't have lied about something

- you shouldn't have cheated on something

- you are getting too close with that guy

- you shouldn't have sent that text ...

They're telling you something you know in your heart you shouldn't be doing, yet you really don't want to hear it from them right now. But, because your friend loves and cares about you, she tells you the truth and it hurts. And the real reason why she even shared with you was because she wants what's best for you: that which brings the kinder side of you out, one that's not selfish and one that's honest. <u>A valued friend is an honest friend!</u>

Baring my soul:

A valued friend is an honest friend ...

Those words remind me of a time when I was honest to a friend, and yet that honesty was not valued at all, and our friendship ended because of it. Let me share ...

When I was in the ninth grade, I started to make new friends; it was the beginning of high school and I was excited and open to finding new friends. There was this one girl whom I befriended that was kind of like the leader of a bunch of us girls that I hung out with. She had a bossy personality and I think we pretty much let her tell us what to do, to not get on her bad side. She was tough and strong, and we figured she could get the better of us if we ever got in a conflict with her. One Friday night, I invited her and four other friends to spend the night at my house. A slumber party in the making, and I was excited for everyone to come over. They all arrived at my house around 5 pm, and we ate dinner and hung out listening to music and looking at the latest teen magazines. Around 7 pm we decided to go outside and go for a little walk in the neighborhood. And as we started to walk down my street a group of guys started walking towards us, and we all started talking, wondering who they were. That is when my bossy friend says, "I know them; one of the guys is my boyfriend." So, I said, "Why are they here?" I did not know them and they did not know me, and they for sure did not know where I lived. And I wondered what they were doing at my house or even on my street. She went on to tell us that she had talked to her boyfriend on the phone earlier, and told him where she would be and that they should come by. I was instantly mad at her that she had invited them all over to my house, and that she had given them my address. I was so mad at her; she should have asked if it was all right for them to come over before she just invited them. Honestly, I didn't want all these guys over, because I was afraid, I would get into trouble with my dad. But my fear started to go away, as all the boys were actually really nice to us and easy to talk with. There were funny jokes going on, we were asking them if they knew other people from each of our different schools, we even compared our schoolwork and homework to theirs—it turned out to be really fun. Then the friend who had invited her boyfriend and his friends over asked if she could go in and use my bathroom; I said of course she could. And as she went in my house her boyfriend came over to me and started talking to me right away, then his talk turned into flirting, and then he asked for my phone number. I said, "Wait a minute, what about my friend? She said you were her boyfriend; I'm not going to do that to her." He told me some lie that they weren't going together anymore and that they were just "good friends," and that was all. Thank God I had enough sense not to give him my phone number ... About twenty more minutes went by and my dad stepped outside and said that us girls needed to come in and that the boys needed to go home. So, we said our good-byes and came into the house. We went into my room and lay all over my bed talking about which boy we thought was cute. Then my friend asked me what I thought of her boyfriend. "Well," I asked her, "are you guys really boyfriend and girlfriend?" She replied, "Yes," and said that he comes over to her house all the time and her mom has met him and really likes him a lot. And then she said they even have kissed before. Okay, so now I knew he was lying to me and that she had no idea what a liar he really was. He was up to no good, by the way he flirted with me … I told her that I thought he was cute, and that made her so happy to think that I thought her boyfriend was cute. That night was the usual sleepover: we stayed up late, talked about everything, and ate junk food. The next day I still felt bad that I did not tell her the truth that this guy she likes tried to pick up on me. The mistake I ended up doing was telling another friend what had happened, and that friend told the bossy friend. (See how gossip works? Even though it's the truth, it's still not good?) Right away this bossy friend called me up on my phone and began yelling at me and telling me that I was the liar and that I was just jealous because she had a cute boyfriend. Once she stopped yelling, I told her the truth of what had happened when she went into the bathroom. She said, "I'm going to talk to him and see what he says." She called me back 15 minutes later and said again that I was a liar and he never asked for my phone number or flirted with me. He was the one who was the liar; of course he didn't tell her the truth because honesty was not part of his character, and she was so bossy she could probably beat him up too. LOL. I said to this bossy friend, "What do I have to gain by making up a lie like that?" I sure did not want him for a boyfriend; I was only trying to save her from a heartache because he was not committed to her. But she did not believe me and ended up telling me that her mom said I couldn't be her friend anymore because I was a liar and a bad influence on her … Wow! It was so far from the truth. But it did end our friendship, and at first it was a little hard because we still both had mutual friends, but a couple months later she ended up leaving and transferring to a different school. You know, with all her bossiness I don't ever remember missing her or her friendship ... That is why I say an honest friend is a valued friend. Or at least an honest friend should be valued.

Please don't ever believe a lie over the truth. If you are not sure what is true in a certain situation, ask God to show you, don't ask other people. People tell lies, and often they tell you what you want to hear, but God always tells us the truth. Jesus says, **"He is the Way, the Truth and the Life"** (John 14:6).

Being a good friend

Let me ask you this: If something embarrassing or maybe a scary thing happened to you, who would be the first friend you would call? Who's someone you could totally trust to be there for you and not let you down? Let's say maybe you started your period at school and you didn't have a pad or tampon. (School is definitely not the best place to start your period. Right?) And let's say you are wearing white pants or light-colored shorts, and now you have a noticeable bloodstain on them. Is there one person you could confide in that could keep this a secret? Is there one friend who would help you get to the school office by giving you a sweatshirt or sweater to tie around your waist, and who wouldn't let anyone else know what was going on? Think about it. Do you have a friend who you could truly trust? How about if I reversed it and I asked you if you were that type of friend that could help another out and keep it a secret? Could someone call on you to help them? That is the kind of friend we need to strive to be, that even when we're tempted to tell, we DON'T! Wouldn't you like to have a friend like that? I sure would! And honestly if I'm going to attract that kind of friend, then I'd better be that kind of friend in return.

"A friend loves at all times," ~Proverbs 17:17 ESV

This scripture clearly says a friend loves <u>all</u> the time. Not some of the times, not when they feel like it times, but <u>all</u> the time. And remember, girls, personal things are <u>always</u> personal ...

Showing grace to our friends

"Dear brothers and sisters, if another believer is overcome by some sin, you who are godly should gently and humbly help that person back onto the right path. And be careful not to fall into the same temptation yourself."
~Galatians 6:1 NLT

This verse means whatever our friends are going through that is hard on them, one day it could be us going through that same problem. So, we need to be extra careful how we act and what we say when we're around our friends. We should treat them the very same way we'd want to be treated. And if we are honest with ourselves, we know we've all messed up before. Right? I know I sure have, and it seems like I continue to do things backwards or in ways I wish I wouldn't ... Seriously!

Jesus example

Do you know what happened on the night before Jesus was crucified? He and His disciples had all just finished dinner, and then Jesus took off His robe, tied a towel around His waist, and began to wash the dirt off the disciples' feet (John 13:1–17). Jesus didn't look at their dirty feet, and say "your feet stink" or "you should really clean your feet!" No, instead, He chose to wash their stinky feet, with no criticism at all ...

Weeds

One day while I was working in my backyard doing some much-needed weeding in my garden, the Lord whispered in my ear, "Even the prettiest gardens grow weeds." It took me a while to understand what God meant by that, but I finally get it ... You see, in a sense we are all like flowers that God cares for in His garden on earth. And every one of us is going to mess up now and then. Weeds are going to pop up in our lives, and some of us are going to get real dirty in this growing process. What do you do when you find out someone you know has gotten dirt on them or has some weeds popping up in their lives? (Meaning their dirt or weeds are their mistakes, either big or small ones.) Are you going to smear their dirt all around, telling everyone you know about it? That would be gossiping and basically squashing their hearts and making them feel like mud. Or are you going to follow Jesus' example, and quietly help wash away their dirt?

Girls, every time we mess up we need to talk to Jesus about it, so He can wash the dirt off us by forgiving us. Remember, none of us are exempt from making mistakes; all of us are going to mess up from time to time—it's a guarantee!

My husband is my best friend, and we have this coffeemaker that lets you set the coffee timer the night before so it will go off early in the morning of the next day. Well, this one time I set the timer, put the coffee in, but had forgotten to put water into the maker. And when my husband got up for work, the timer went off but no coffee was made because it had no water in it ... (Blonde moment. ☺) But you know something, he didn't get all mad at me, he knew I just messed up and forgot the water. That's it, and that's what makes a good friend—they understand and show us grace when we mess up. ☺ They see our dirt and our mistakes and love us anyways. So, let's stop pointing fingers at others and start pointing our fingers back at ourselves, because one day it's likely that we will be leaving the dirty and muddy footprints left behind ...

May I ask, where are you at this very moment? Are you rubbing the mud in about someone else, or are you like Jesus, lovingly washing it off someone?

Let's Review- Never make fun of others or ridicule them.

- Let your friends know you love them and accept them.

- Don't be phony, be genuine.

- Most people retaliate when they are hurt by another person. So, the best way to avoid these attacks is to stay away from gossiping, mean looks, hurtful words, or cruel texts.

- Being kind and sincere to others will bring you personally more joy.

- You will be surprised by how you will attract good friends when you are caring and understanding, when you love others when they make mistakes, and when you stand up for them when others are trying to make them look bad.

A true friend is one who will always be there for you when no one else will. When everyone else walks out the door they walk in.

For the hurting heart

Maybe right now you feel really sad, let down, like you're not being treated fairly by some friend or friends ... Know this: God is watching <u>everything</u>! Not only does God hear everything but He sees it all. Jesus tells us that He sees every sparrow that falls to the ground, and how much more valuable you are than many sparrows (Matthew 10:28–31). Jesus is watching everything, and because of how loving He is, I just know that He has a plan to work all that you are going through all out for good one day (see Romans 8:28).

Please, please hang in there.

May these next words sink into your hearts …**Man's rejection is often God's protection.**

That means when your friends abandon you, it's highly likely that God is protecting you.

> Jesus tells you right now, **"the one who comes to Me, I will by no means cast away."** ~John 6:37

Jesus truly is our Faithful Friend! Talk to Him, and choose to hang out with Him. I promise He will never walk away from you, or turn His back on you—not ever!

Prayer:

Dear Jesus,

Help me to forgive the one girl who bugs me the most. Help me to forgive her faults as You remind me of my own faults and dirt in my life. Thank you for always being there for me, through all my tears. Help me to be a good friend and also to have good friends; thank you.

Amen.

CHAPTER 2

Popularity

I don't know about you, but the subject of popularity sure gets my attention. ☺

I like knowing who are the popular actors and actresses, who's on the top charts in music, along with the best sports stars. The recognition they all get, the fame, the pictures, the interviews, the attention, it all looks so glamorous, and for a lot of us girls, like me, it causes us to dream and wish that we could get recognized and become popular—well, at least one time in our lives, or maybe, just to get a little taste of popularity. Right? I do know this: that along with all the high points and attention one gets, there can also be some really low points in being popular too. Let me give you a personal example of what I'm talking about.

True Story

Back in the tenth grade I wanted to hang out with the cool crowd or with the popular crowd, and I ended up leaving behind my best friend because she wasn't cool or popular. I just didn't think I would be popular if I had a "nobody knows who they are" type of friend.

Yet, when I think back about my friend, she was always there for me whenever I needed to talk to someone, we had lots of fun together, and she admired and looked up to me. I don't know about you, but I tend to think that's what we all really want or crave in being popular; it's about being admired and looked up to. The friend I left behind was the one who got me involved into church and Bible study, and she also introduced me to my future husband. We even started cosmetology school together, but she ended up dropping out of beauty school. Beauty school dropout ... there is a song in the movie *Grease* called "Beauty School Dropout." Sometimes I wonder if I had anything to do with my friend dropping out of beauty school??? ... Honestly, I just wasn't a good friend to her, and today I still feel bad for how I treated her ...

You see, I wanted more ... When all along I had enough!

That's one of the main reasons why I share with you my personal stories; it's because I wish I could keep you from all the mistakes I've made. I've caused a lot of pain in my search for popularity ...

I remember giving dirty looks to girls just based on how they looked. I'm so ashamed and embarrassed to admit that, but it's true. The shame of gossiping about another person just to make them look bad, when all along they were innocent. Being quick to tease someone if they made a mistake, kind of like I was always on the hunt to find someone failing or making a mistake so I could laugh at them. You could say it was like an immature game that I and some of my friends played, looking to put another person down. Doesn't that sound ridiculous and horrible? Not to mention selfish and self-centered. There was a time in my life I was a mean girl. I think in some twisted way I thought if I put others down it would make me look better ... And that makes no sense, yet it stemmed from my own insecurities. I truly thought in a twisted or warped way, it definitely wasn't right. I am so ashamed and embarrassed to think how mean

I was. I was <u>not</u> treating others how I wanted to be treated—that's for sure—and that's the incredibly sad truth.

True Story #2

I remember another time I was at a church youth group barbeque and swim party. Everyone always had a lot of fun at this house because this family had the coolest and biggest pool, an outdoor kitchen area, and an indoor sauna to get all nice and warm in when the pool water felt too chilly. So, there I was with my little clique of Christian friends, and of course the ones I hung out with just happened to be the coolest … Go figure, right? I always wanted to be with the "in crowd." We were all eating and playing games and talking and hanging out, and in walks through the backyard this girl that we all thought was weird—I think her name was Carry. All of us popular girls felt like the only thing Carry had going for her was her name, as Carry sounded kind of cute. But … Carry was far from cute to me and to my friends. Whenever Carry would come by us "cliquey" girls, we ended up having an excuse and left when she came near. A bunch of guys were playing ball in the pool so she decided to join the guys in the pool, since us girls wouldn't give her the time of day. That's a figure of speech, but I think you know what I'm saying. Carry began to take off her t-shirt and then started to take her shorts off; she had worn her bathing suit under her regular clothes. Well, anyways, as she took off her shorts and was left standing in her bathing suit, immediately all of us girls noticed something different, and rather than one of us having kindness in our hearts to intervene and help her out, we all laughed at her and got even more disgusted with her. I seriously feel so bad when I tell you what the problem was. You see, Carry hadn't ever shaved around her bikini line before, and she had a lot of black pubic hair that grew down the upper inside of her legs that stuck out past her bikini line. It stuck out of her bathing suit, and in a bad way. So much so, that it was very noticeable. Oh, the shame I feel for not doing the right thing, for not showing her any kindness. Instead, I was with a group of girls that humiliated her. ☹ I was not acting at the time like Jesus lived in my heart; nor were my friends. I think my actions were cruel in how I treated Carry. Sigh ... ☹ Come to find out later I had heard that Carry's mom had died when she was a little girl and her dad was raising her all on his own. I also heard that they didn't have much money and struggled just to have food for dinner. Oh, the shame I live with being such a snob, the "mean girl," as I lived out my pursuit of being popular ...

Side Note

If you need to shave your bikini line, please don't be embarrassed. I shave my bikini area, and to be honest, so do most girls and women. ;) Truth!

Sometimes we think that the cute guys won't notice us if we are hanging out with the nerdy people or the ordinary people. But honestly, guys will notice you with whomever you are with. Guys have what I call "Guy-radar," and their eyes seem to spot any and every girl within a 100-yard radius. ☺ And it may be even easier on the guy to come talk with you if he doesn't think everyone is watching him. Like if you are hanging out with the popular kids then all eyes are watching that crowd, and that may be more intimidating for some guys to walk up to you and start a conversation with you then.

You see, sometimes we seek after beautiful friends, rather than friends with beautiful hearts ...

Two Types of Beauty in Women

There are two types of beauty in a woman. Her **external beauty** and her **internal beauty**. And I believe it's God's desire for us to live out both of them in a beautiful way.

EXTERNAL BEAUTY – Is how we look naturally, and we can always enhance ourselves with makeup, clothes, and by our hairstyles. External beauty does not last. It's kind of like a beautiful flower that dies shortly after we pick it. Time, gravity, and just plain living out our everyday lives has a way of changing all our external beauty.

INTERNAL BEAUTY – Is what God looks at, and this beauty is made clear to the people we are the closest to. It's a sweet spirit that is loving, kindhearted, forgiving, and compassionate. It's also what we all want in our friends. And it's those character traits of internal beauty that Jesus longs to develop in all of us … It's not like external beauty where it fades; our internal beauty should get prettier and prettier throughout all the years of our lives.

> **"Don't be concerned about the outward beauty of fancy hairstyles, expensive jewelry, or beautiful clothes. You should clothe yourselves instead with the beauty that comes from within, the unfading beauty of a gentle and quiet spirit, which is so precious to God."** ~I Peter 3:3–4 NLT

Peter describes this beauty as a gentle and quiet spirit; this also means being calm and being free from irritations. I'm convinced without question as a girl that this is our most powerful quality: a gentle spirit. And this beauty comes from deep inside you, from your hidden person, who you are in your heart. **Who you really are …**

When you think about it, our outward appearance doesn't take all that long to perfect. We know how to get ready fast when we have to. We've all seen women in their cars driving while putting on mascara and blush. One time, I even saw a woman brushing her teeth while she was driving (I have no idea where she chose to spit her toothpaste out at. LOL! ☺) Truth is, as girls we can get ready anywhere and in just about any way. When we have a deadline, we know how to get ready fast!

But, girls, all our external beauty will fade and pass by us one day—all of ours will ... Yet, it will take a lifetime to prepare and develop the hidden person of our hearts. You just can't put a rush on your inner beauty ...

People go to extreme measures to enhance their external beauty, in their pursuit of fitting in or becoming popular. They put their bodies through a vast array of cosmetic surgeries to fix and enhance everything, as they aim for what our society or culture says is the prettiest. They will have face-lifts, Botox injections, lip injections, nose jobs, teeth perfection, breast implants; they have their bottoms fixed (called Brazilian butts); they have stomach surgeries taking out ribs to make their waist super tiny; and now women are getting tattoos as makeup, as eyeliner, lipstick, and eyebrows. (I'm thinking of getting my eyebrows done.) There are also hair extensions and eyelash extensions. (I personally may like the eyelash extensions too—just being real. LOL. ☺) There are probably lots more tricks and surgeries that I don't even know about—lots more! Most models these days are not "all" natural, or like how God first created them.

Yes, people will go through drastic measures to rebuild their outside bodies. But you know what? No surgeon can work miracles on a person's internal beauty, or the inside of a person's heart and make it beautiful. Only God can perform surgery on our inner hearts, and again that's the place where the real us lives. Oh, how we need to quit trying to be people pleasers, and instead work on being God pleasers. My hope is that you will not lose your true self just to be popular …

There was a man in the Bible who was guilty of wanting to please the crowd; his name was Pontius Pilate. He wanted to win the popular vote and keep the people happy, so he chose not to listen to what God was speaking to him in his heart, and he ended up pleasing the crazy crowd. I think Pilate knew what the right thing to do was, but instead, he chose to listen to the voice of the crowd. And we all know where the voice of the crowd led him: "Crucify Him! Crucify Him!" (Matthew 27:22–23) How tragic it is when any of us give in to the loud voice of the crowd, instead of obeying the still, small voice of God … I'm sooo guilty of not listening to God's sweet voice at times in my own life …

"You must not follow the crowd in doing wrong."
~Exodus 23:2 NLT

God spoke those words to the children of Israel many years ago. Yet, His voice still speaks the same to us today. We must be willing to be kind, honest, and truthful even if everyone else is doing the opposite. It's not as hard to know what the right thing to do is, as it is to do the right thing. Let me repeat that. **It is not as hard to know what the right thing to do is, as it is to do the right thing.** In other words, the hard part is following through in doing the right thing. The way to greatness is simply to say, "Regardless of what others do, I'm going to do what I know is pleasing to God."

True Story #3

Back when I was in junior high school there was this girl whose name was Angie, and she was cool because she wasn't afraid to be different. She liked Elton John a lot (if you don't know who Elton John is do a Google search on him to see how he looks), to the point that she would dress like him. Every day at school she would wear big sunglasses, platform shoes, and long tails on a dress-tux coat. She even would put sparkles on her face and put them in her hair (this was before it was in style). One day we found out there was going to be a big talent show at our school. And you guessed it, Angie was going to do a couple of songs that Elton John sang. We all wondered what kind of voice she would have. On that day, the auditorium was packed, and we couldn't wait to hear Angie sing. When it came to her turn, she had cool lights flashing, sparkles everywhere, the music was cranked up super loud, and Angie came out in the highest platform heels I ever saw. But when our eyes left all the special effects that were taking place on the stage and looked to Angie, we noticed in shock that she wasn't really singing. I think our mouths dropped open with disappointment as we realized Angie was just lip-singing to an Elton John song called "Crocodile Rock." What a letdown to know she was just faking to sing like him. Although she did a good job pretending to play the piano and sing like Elton John, we all walked out a bit disappointed, as we thought she of all people might have been a real talent. Instead she was just imitating someone famous. And that is what a lot of popular people are like: they're just good at imitating ...

No matter where you go there will always be popular people. You might even be popular right now, and in a year or two you won't be ... Or maybe you never will be popular in school, but one day as an adult you will be (you are like a diamond in the rough). *It always seems that "who's who" today will be "who cares" tomorrow ... That's how it is with popularity and fame—it just doesn't last ...

And let me remind you that there is a lot of responsibility that comes with being popular, especially as a Christian, or as Jesus' daughter.

You see if we act, and look, like how our culture wants us to look, then what happens is people get bored seeing the same thing over and over. Seriously, when we all act the same then others yawn, and stretch their arms out really wide; they take deep breaths and then sigh, then they get tired of watching us and they look away. B-u-t-t-t, if we look different and we don't wear clothes that our society is dictating for us to wear, if our actions are different, if our words are different, if we smile and are happy, then all of a sudden people take notice from their bored state and they find themselves wondering, "Why are they so different???"

Girls, stand out in a good way, in a different way; my hope is that it will be in a way that pleases God.

When people look at you, what do they see?

- Do they see the good things you do?

- Do they see you smile?

- Do they hear kindness in your voice?

- Do they notice you say "thank you" to others?

- Do they hear you apologize when you are wrong?

Plain and simple, do they see Jesus in you???

Baring my soul:

When I was about 13 years old I did something so bad that it still makes my heart sad when I think about it ... Here goes ... There was girl in our neighborhood who was six years older than me; I used to hang out at her house in the summer because they had a swimming pool and all the kids liked to swim there. This girl was so beautiful, I admired her so much and wanted to look and dress just like she did. She was popular and older than me so I looked up to her. Well, this one day she was going to go to the mall and she asked me if I wanted to go with her. Wow! You bet I wanted to go—I couldn't wait! So, we arrived at the mall and boy did I think I was cool wearing my best ditto jeans with a cute top on, and with a pretty, "older-than-me friend" who could drive. Life was exciting and cool! We went to her favorite clothing store and she found some clothes to try on, so we went into the dressing rooms together. I was like her helper. We had a buddy system: I would rehang the clothes after she tried them on. And as we got into this dressing room, I looked at this shelf that was meant to put purses on, and lying on the shelf was a necklace. My older friend said to me, "Someone must have left it in here, go ahead and put it in your wallet in the chain part and keep it." "Finders keepers, losers, weepers," she said. I did not like that idea and I told her, "No, you keep it." She said something like "I can't" because she was busy trying on clothes right now, but when we left, she would get it from me. I did what she asked me to do but hated doing it. About five minutes later someone knocked on the dressing room door. "Excuse me," came a voice. My friend said, "Yes, I'm in this room, do you need something?" This lady went on to say she left her necklace on the shelf and could she please have it back? This lady had a really nice voice. And my friend said, "Where did you leave it?" And when the lady described where it was (exactly where I picked it up from) she says back to her, "No, I don't see any necklace, maybe someone was in here before us." I'm hitting her on the leg saying, "No way," mouthing, "We have to give it back to her," and she is telling me no strongly back. I was beginning to sweat. Then the lady says, "Please, it's got to be in there, I was just in there." I about died. I'm lipping to my friend, "We must give it back to this woman," and she is lipping, back to me, "No, it's too late." The lady left, and when we walked out of the dressing room this lady had the security guard waiting for us. The security guard talked with my friend and she was adamant that she had no necklace; she paid for her clothes and we walked out of that store and back into the main mall. The security guard followed us for a little way further into the mall, then we walked out of the mall and headed back to her car. As soon as we were in her car, I took out that necklace and said that this was wrong and that I could never keep this and I so wished that would have never happened. She went on to say that once she'd denied not seeing the necklace, then she couldn't say then that she found it to the lady. I thought to myself, whatever?!? I honestly wished I would never have ever gone to the mall that day with the coolest person—so I'd thought she was. Because my admiration of her changed real, quick! I knew what the right thing was to do, but I didn't do it ... That's what pursuing popularity did for me: made me into a liar and a thief! I still feel the shame of that today ... ☹

TV stars, sports stars, famous rock stars, and movie stars—people whom we admire and look up to sometimes start off seeming like really good people, but a lot of times they fall short of deserving our respect, just like my girlfriend, did. We need to be careful that those who we are following know where they are going ...

*Truly, girls, the key to greatness and great things is hanging out and around Jesus.

His ways are brilliant, honest, gracious, truthful, and exceptionally kind. ...

Humility

One thing that must come in all our lives, especially with being popular, is humility, or staying humble. For a popular person, being humble means not always being so talkative, taking a back seat rather than a front seat, not being noticed—all of these are very difficult for a popular person to live out.

Criticism

And here's something to think about that I bet you didn't know: being criticized could truly, actually be good for us. Now I know what you are thinking ... I hate being criticized too, but it truly can stop us from going down the wrong road or roads. I wish someone would have criticized me back when I was putting a necklace that did not belong to me in my wallet!

Jesus is our Example:

When we think of Jesus, we could say so many wonderful things about Him with all His amazing character qualities: He's loving, giving, caring, kind, gracious, longsuffering, forgiving, patient—the list could literally go on and on. But you know what? In the Bible Jesus describes Himself in only two ways. It's true; listen to what they are:

> **"Take My yoke upon you. Let me teach you, because I am humble and gentle at heart, and you will find rest for your souls."** ~Matthew 11:29 NLT

Can you say these are characteristics of you? Are you gentle and are you humble? Solomon, the wisest king who ever lived, said, **"let another person praise you ... a stranger, and not your own lips"** (Proverbs 27:2 NLT).

Plainly put, let others brag about you, don't brag about yourself!

Cute Story

Several little kids were playing with a big brown box. And one of the little kids said, "I know, let's make a clubhouse out of this box." So, as they were cutting out holes for windows and doors, one of the other kids said, "Let's write on one of these scraps of cardboard the clubhouse rules." They all decided what the rules would be.

Clubhouse Rules:

#1) No one act big.

#2) No one act small.

#3) Everyone act medium.

I like that! Just act medium. Now that's wisdom!

> **"Don't be selfish; don't try to impress others. Be humble, thinking of others as better than yourselves. Don't look out only for your own interests, but take an interest in others, too."** ~Philippians 2:3–4 NLT

In other words, just act medium! Honestly, when we try to act big, we usually are left disappointed because we soon find out there is always someone bigger and better than us ...

My Dream:

One night I had a really scary dream. I dreamt that I was turning into some type of a reptile—a snake is what it seemed like to me. My skin was getting all tight and scaly, my hair was falling out, and my eyes were tightening, like I was squinting. Truly I was getting super ugly fast! And through my whole dream I kept thinking of the verse:

"People judge by outward appearance, but the Lord looks at the heart."
~I Samuel 16:7 NLT

In my dream there would be friends who would come over and visit with me, and some of them couldn't even look at me because of my ugliness. I was so scary looking! Yet, some of my friends who would concentrate on looking at my eyes, and looking deep into them, found something familiar in me. And as they looked deeply into my eyes, I knew then that they were my true friends, because they were willing to look beyond my horribly ugly outside body; they chose to look at my heart, my internal beauty ...

What if?

What if we all became blind, and we couldn't see anything anymore? I believe then we would get past the outward looks of everyone's clothes, hair, makeup, their whole fashion, and our ears would take over. And as we listened to how people acted and what they said, we would see how people really are. And I think that's how God truly wants us to see people: by looking beyond just what's on the outside ...

"Jesus says, I entered this world to render judgement—to give sight to the blind and to show those who think they see that they are blind."
~John 9:39 NLT

The World Values

- Beauty

- Intelligence

- Fame

God Hates What the World Values!

> Then he said to them, "You like to appear righteous in public, but God knows your hearts. What the world honors is detestable in the sight of God."
> ~Luke 16:15 NLT

I've heard it said before that "show-offs love saying sugary and syrupy words." Things like, "I like your hair, your shirt, your backpack, your car ..." Sometimes we really do mean them and other times it's "syrupy," meaning it's phony. It's flattery, and most of the time flattery isn't sincere or honest.

Yes, at times our talk is phony; we say flattering words only to sound good to other people in hopes to impress them. But you know what? We can't fool God—we just can't! And on top of that, the Lord always talks straight and truthful to us; He is very clear and precise with no phoniness ever. And God's truthful words are plainly written in black and white throughout our bibles. Truth!

Copycats

Does it ever bug you when people copy you?

When I was young my friends and I used to ride our bikes all around the block in our neighborhood, and as we rode, we would pretend that our bikes were our cars. We would shout out and say, "I'm driving a Corvette," and then someone else would say, "I have a Porsche; we each would try to out-trump the other's type of car that we pretended to have. Well, somehow, it always turned out (maybe because I could think of a lot, more different types of cars than my friends) that they would end up mimicking me all the time with pretend cars. If I had a Porsche then they had a Porsche, and if I had a Corvette then they had one; a Mustang, they had one, a Volkswagen bug, yep, they had one too. So, this one day I thought I'd be real, clever and say I was a taxi. My friends thought that also sounded great, so they were taxis as well. Oh, how it used to make me so mad that I couldn't be original, that they always had to copy me … But you know what? Now I understand and realize that it's a true compliment when people try to copy me, and the same is true when they try to copy you as well. It's truly one of the nicest types of compliments! It means they admire your style. Don't let it bug you when people copy you. Just concentrate on setting good trends for others to follow. ☺

Be You

Now, the popular kids usually set what is cool. But I say to you, like what you like and be who you are! John the Baptist was not that cool to look at, and he ate bugs—ew! Yet he lived to please God, and people flocked to him all the time to be baptized. They say that the happiest people are not the ones who have the <u>most</u>, but the ones who need the <u>least</u>. That was John the Baptist: he didn't need much!

You know something? You don't have to be a follower. Maybe God made you to be a leader … There was a movie out a while ago called

What a Girl Wants; Amanda Bynes starred in it (chick flick). Well anyways, there is a line in that movie that has always stuck with me. Amanda in character is crying out to this guy she likes telling him her problems, and he says to her (I love this part), "Why are you trying to fit in, when you were meant to stand out?"

So, I say this to some of you:

WHY ARE YOU TRYING TO FIT IN WHEN YOU WERE MEANT TO STAND OUT?

Stick true to your heart. Be who God made you to be. Let's say you and your friends go into an ice-cream shop, and all your friends want to get some type of chocolate-flavored ice cream, yet, everything in you is saying, "No, I want the best ice cream in the world: Sweet Cream!" (Which to me is like the greatest vanilla ice cream I've ever tasted.) But, you end up getting a chocolate-flavored ice cream because all your friends got chocolate and you didn't want to be different than them. And now every time you put a bite of ice cream into your mouth you are so disappointed, because you really wanted the flavor of Sweet Cream ... That's why I say to you, stick to what you like, be you! And who knows ... maybe next year everyone will be looking to you to see what flavor of ice cream you will be picking out. ☺

Serious thoughts:

Do you ever say to yourself, "I'm worthless? I can never do anything right!" Well, that is a lie—it's just not true! You might feel like a loser sometimes, you might even be called a loser by those around you, but they are LIES! The fact that God chooses you makes you a winner! We need to realize that everyone who calls Jesus Lord, regardless of her personality or popularity or looks, is a winner because they have been chosen by Him. Jesus picked you to be on His team! God says to us at times when we feel like rejects, "Follow Me, I will always choose you, others might be mean to you, turn their backs on you, and avoid you, but I am willing to work with you and work in you. You are special to Me." Oh, how God speaks the sweetest words!

In Closing

Are you inspired for nothing or are you inspired for something? **Nothing** is what the world wants you to be. **Something** is what God wants you to be ... And we find peace knowing God loves us just the way we are right now ...

Review

Are people happy to see you when you walk into the room or are they happier to see you leave the room? Think about that one ...

We desire all the time to have relationships with popular and famous people. But there is only **ONE** who is truly much more beyond famous. His name is Jesus! He is the One we should admire, desire, and want to take after ...

Girls, live your life for Jesus. I like to say, live like the Little Drummer Boy in that familiar Christmas song.

- Come to Him

- Play for Him

- Do your best for Him

And then, He smiles at you ... That is the best part in this entire world: to have Jesus smile at you ... drum roll please ...

Prayer:

Dear Lord,

Thank you for believing in me, even when I don't believe in myself. Jesus, thank you that you can take a plain and ordinary girl and do something extraordinary with her.

I love You, amen.

CHAPTER 3

The Subject is Boys /
The Character is Modesty

Boys-Boys-Boys ...

I'd like to start this chapter by listing all the boys I have liked since the age of five years old. Here goes ...

K-5 Nathan – I met him in kindergarten; he had super-blond-white hair and he wore his hair in a short buzz haircut. He was sweet and shy like most kindergarten boys are. One day in class the teacher gave us a contest, the boys against the girls, to see who was the fastest at untying knots in a rope. The side who finished first would win. It was down to me for the girls and Nathan for the boys and I ended up beating him. I got done way faster than he did untying the knots in the girl's rope. Yay! But I broke his heart in doing so, because he got beat by a girl. Yeah, that was me ...

1st grade – Keith – He was Nathan's brother. And he was not shy in the least. He asked for my phone number on the first day of school in first grade, and I, not knowing any better, gave him my number. He ended up calling me after school that same day, and boy, did I get a talking to from my mom; she was furious that I gave a boy my phone number! I was so young, and I thought it would impress Keith by having my phone number memorized. I learned quickly not to give my phone number out to just anyone!

2nd grade – Brian – He was just really cute! He was the one that a—l—l the girl's thought was cute! There is always a guy like that. Right?

3rd grade – Steve – He again was just really cute; I mean really cute! He had dark brown hair and the prettiest green eyes, and the longest, thickest eyelashes I've ever seen. Why do the guys always get the longest eyelashes???

4th grade – David – Just cute again. And he was really good at sports. When picking teams for dodgeball, everyone always picked David first.

5th & 6th grade – David – This David was a different David than from fourth grade; he was very strong, good in sports, easy to talk to, and just super nice to me—he would even stick up for me when others teased me. Although David teased me too, somehow it just seemed like a flirty tease from him, like how a good friend would joke around with you.

7th grade – Frank – He was super nice, shy but easy to talk to. He had dark brown hair and beautiful blue eyes. I remember he would call me at home, and in junior high it was cool having guys call me. We had the same taste in music, and we could talk for an easy hour on the phone about the songs and bands we liked.

8th grade – Scott – He was my first real boyfriend. He got many kisses from me. Oh, how I wish that wasn't true …

9th grade – Nobody ... (I met this guy named Tim at a youth group barbeque. He liked me I could tell, but I didn't like him. I didn't think he was cute ... ha-ha.)

10th grade – Nobody ...

11th, 12th grade – Tim Young – You guessed it! I fell for him and we got married shortly after I graduated from high school. I didn't stand a chance, because I found out he had been praying for me ... Guess God maybe had something to do with us falling for each other?

My point through all of this is that we change a lot and so does our taste in the guys we like. Don't worry if that guy doesn't like you right now, it's not the end of the world (even though it might feel like it); he's probably not the guy God has planned for you to marry anyways ... Or maybe, like me, the <u>one</u> you don't think is cute right now, will one day steal your heart away.

If I were to ask any group of girls, how many of you have ever thought a guy was cute, every hand would be in the air. Right? We've all thought a guy was cute before—every one of us has. That is the way God made us. Boys are naturally attracted to girls and girls to guys. It's part of God's design. However, we need to have our priorities in order when we start liking guys.

"Seek the kingdom of God above all else, and live righteously, and he will give you everything you need." ~Matthew 6:33 NLT

God wants us to look to Him first before anything else or before anyone else. Trust me on this; He knows that if we put a guy, or a friend, or a TV show, or a sport, or music group, or a hobby or any of those types of things before Him, we will end up not happy in the end. Jesus is the only one who can truly fill our hearts and minds with the best of love, joy, and peace that all of us girls crave. And you know something? When you get to the point of putting Jesus first, or asking Him what you should do in any situation, then you will find that He has a way of making all of your deep-down desires really come true.

> **"... the hopes of the godly will be granted"**
> ~Proverbs 10:24b NLT

That means when you are actively talking with Jesus and listening to Him, He will be faithful to take care of all your hopes and your heart's desires ...

I want you to read this next verse out loud if you would. Listen carefully to what the words say as you read it out loud.

> **"And so, dear sisters, I plead with you to give your bodies to God because of all he has done for you. Let them be a living and holy sacrifice—the kind he will find acceptable. This is truly the way to worship him. Don't copy the behavior and customs of the world, but let God transform you into a new person by changing the way you think. Then you will learn to know God's will for you, which is good and pleasing and perfect."** ~Romans 12:1–2 NLT

What a beautiful verse! Read it over several times until you get the gist of what it's asking of us ... We are always to be representing God with our bodies in a way that honors Him.

Let's talk about modesty:

Do you know what it means to be modest? If we were to look up the word "modesty" in the dictionary or by Googling it, it would read something like this: <u>modesty</u> – to dress with reason; being re-strained; not extreme; having good behavior in the way they dress; or hidden elegance. I LOVE that definition: "hidden elegance ..." Let that stick and sink into your thoughts, because it sure has captured my thoughts and my mind. "**Hidden Elegance.**" So beautiful!!!

Now if we head in the opposite direction of being modest, we get a word called "<u>pretentious</u>"; "pretentious" means daring and showy. And from "pretentious" we get another word called "<u>ambitious</u>"; "ambitious" means having ambition. So, we could say if a person is not modest in the way they dress, then they are:

<u>Daring</u> – By maybe wearing clothes that are too short, or too tight, or too low cut;

<u>Showy</u> – Maybe showing too much skin on their bodies; and

<u>Ambitious</u> – having a goal in mind in how they dress.

What is a pretentious girl's goal, you might ask? It is simply to at-tract attention, mostly from guys ...

> **"A pretentious showy life is an empty life; a plain and simple life is a full life."** ~Proverbs 13:7 MSG

Serious subject

Girls, may I ask you something just between you and me? What do you think the boys are thinking about when you are wearing short skirts or short-shorts, or too low of a cut of pants (to the point of where your butt or underwear is showing), or wearing a top so low-cut or see-through that it shows off your breasts? I think I know what you are probably thinking: maybe something like, that guy's noticing you and he thinks you look super cute or pretty or trendy, or hot. Right? And may I also assume that you like it when guys look at you. Am I right again? You are not alone if you think that way; most of us girls do. But, there's a very serious side to all this pretentious showiness. And I want to be super honest and real with you right now: when those guys are checking you out, "cute" and "pretty" are not the only thoughts you are causing those guys to think about you when you are wearing outfits that lack modesty. Honestly, most likely those boys are battling with lustful thoughts of you, and in their imaginations, they are secretly undressing you all the way, even past your bras and underwear. Some are even going further and imagining that they are having sex with you. If I had the chance to meet you and talk with you about this subject, you would probably tell me very quickly that this is not what you want them to do. It's probably unimaginable to you that this is what is happening. But that is what is happening every time you wear an outfit that lacks modesty. Even the good Christian guys that you think are so sweet and nice and caring, they too struggle with sexual thoughts, lust, especially when they see a girl dressing sexy.

True Story

One day, when I was sitting in my car stopped at a red light looking in my rearview mirror, I saw a man driving a minivan that was coming up from behind me. He pulled over to the curb and let a young girl out of the car. Something just didn't sit right with me as to why he would drop her off at the curb on a busy street: no parent would drop off their teenager where this guy dropped her off at, it just wasn't a safe area. Out came this young girl from the van and she walked away. I soon realized that by the way she acted and the expression on her face she was probably a prostitute. And do you know what this young girl was wearing? She was wearing a cropped top and low-cut blue blue-jeans, just like what's in most of the clothing stores in the mall. Just like what you might even like to wear, and maybe even is hanging in your closet ... You know, it used to be that years ago, everyone knew who the prostitutes were just by how they dressed. And nowadays fashion is dictating for us girls to wear clothes that lack modesty, the same that are in a prostitute's wardrobe. Truly I believe there should be a difference in what we wear so it doesn't give the opinion to guys that we are easily available for the right price. I hope you get what I'm saying ...

Honestly, guys will find a way to look at you no matter what you are wearing. You don't need to give them skin or anything else for them to notice you ... In fact, one time I was in a grocery store wearing a pair of sandals with my new color of orange toenail polish on. And a man walked right up to me and said that I had the sexiest toes he ever saw. Wow!!! Now my toes are an object of sexiness. See what I mean??? Guys will look at you even if you are in sweatpants and a sweatshirt. ☺

Let's be honest

Tell me, do you really feel comfortable wearing clothes that are too revealing? Don't you think having to pull up, or pull down, or push up is just too much work? I know I sure do. I hate having to worry about my clothes. What we wear has a way of telling others how we are. If we wear clothes that are, let's say, sexy, then we are telling others that we like to be sexy. But the problem with dressing sexy is, it tells guys that you are somewhat interested in having sex with them. Did you realize that? That's what dressing sexy displays. Girls, I don't want you to be ashamed of the clothes you wear. Please don't let our culture get the pleasure of telling what you should wear based upon what is in fashion and what the "in-crowd" is saying is cool to wear. You can still be trendy by being creative and dressing modestly. Try to improvise the latest styles by thinking outside of the box of fashion, and add something to cover the areas the world wants you to show off. Like maybe a scarf, a jacket, leggings, a necklace, a skirt or shirt. There are no regrets when we dress modestly.

Accountability

*Remember, not only do you pull yourself down when your outfits aren't modest, but you pull guys down too. Did you know that? And you also are pulling your girlfriends down with you, because they could be looking to you to see what's cool to wear. You see, our culture tells you and me to do whatever makes us feel good. That we're not responsible if others struggle with the way we dress. Right? Wrong! God says something totally different than what our society says.

> **"Don't look out only for your own interests, but take an interest in others, too."** ~Philippians 2:4 NLT

Dressing modestly is not only a good choice for you; but it shows you care and have concern for others too. Like your friends, for instance, and the guys around you ...

China Teacup Versus a Styrofoam Cup

The way you present yourself to a guy is how he will treat you. Start presenting yourself to guys like you are a **Beautiful China Teacup**. You are very valuable, priceless to be exact, fragile, and one who needs to be treated with great care. Or you could present yourself like a **Cheap Styrofoam Cup**. You don't show your value to others, you are easily available, can be used and then crushed and thrown in the trash. Sad but so true. Choose to be like a china teacup; you are valuable and very priceless. There is only one you in this whole wide world—that makes you very special!

Your heart is a treasure, and you should offer it to someone who is mature enough to handle your heart well ...

So often, we think God is concerned about our reputation, but, He is more concerned with your overall character. Our reputation is what and who others think we are. Our character is who we really are. There are those who have a great reputation in the sight of others, but their character is sadly lacking. And there are also those whose reputation may have had some problems (maybe from a false accusation), but their character is pure and honest. Who you are deep down even when no one is looking at you—that's your true character. And there's no hiding anything from God: He knows who we really are.

3 Words to Remember

<u>Morality</u> – meaning: principles of right and wrong

<u>Chastity</u> – meaning: having self-control or self-restraint by refraining from sex

<u>Virginity</u> – meaning: never to have had sex before

Some people think "Big deal"; who cares if I lose my virginity before I get married? I'll tell you who cares—God does! And "**The Big Deal**" is God clearly says NO SEX outside of marriage!

> **"God's will is for you to be holy, so stay away from all sexual sin."**
> ~I Thessalonians 4:3 NLT

God warns us to stay away from all sexual sin; that means God wants you to keep your virginity until you are married.

Girls, God is not some mean God that doesn't want you to be happy, He only tells us no for our own good, to protect us. If only we could grasp hold of the reality that His plans are WAY better for us than anything we could ever imagine or anything that we could ever plan for ourselves! There is a verse in my Bible that I have written the word "dream" next to. Listen to what it says.

"Now all glory to God, who is able, through his mighty power at work within us, to accomplish infinitely more than we might ask or think."
~Ephesians 3:20 NLT

My interpretation of this scripture is that God is capable in every way of blessing us much more than what we could ever dream or imagine for ourselves! God loves us so much that His plans, His dreams for us, are sooo much better than what our own imaginations can dream up. So, if God tells me "no," it's because He has something WAY better in mind for me … Trust Him in all that you go through, even when everything in you is screaming yes, I want to do this, and God is saying, "No." Always listen to His voice and to His Word over yours every time. Let His thoughts trump your thoughts. It's all about surrendering to His will before our own wills. The day that you realize God's dreams for you are SO much better than what you could ever dream for yourself, is the day you will begin to grow beautiful roots of faith deep down in your hearts.

God created you; He knows what you like and need

You and I have been made by God, for God. Our hearts have a carved-out hole in them that aches to be filled with God's love. Everything about you and me God created, and because He designed us, He uniquely knows us best. He knows exactly what you and I really need all the time. Relationships, all the things about guys and feelings towards them are great. As a matter of fact, they can be wonderful! It's just that <u>all</u> those feelings and thoughts by themselves will never fill you up completely, and they will never be enough to make you truly happy and feel complete. Apart from Jesus there will always be emptiness in your heart. So, a boyfriend truly can be a wonderful thing and a sweet blessing, but only when your heart is full of love towards Jesus first. For you will always feel incomplete if you expect a guy to fill up the holes in your heart that <u>only God was meant to fill</u>.

<u>Chastity</u> means pure in thoughts and actions and even your intentions.

True Story

One day, a friend shared with me how her daughter saw some really good girls at a party dancing very sexy, or in a flirtatious way. There's an old name for this type of dancing; it's called "Dirty Dancing." (Ever seen the movie called *Dirty Dancing*? If you haven't I bet your mom has. ☺) These girls were super sweet and they loved God, yet, they danced in a way that they shouldn't be proud of; it was provocative, and not chaste. When I heard about this story, it really bothered me because I personally knew these girls, and loved them, so I prayed to Jesus, asking Him with real tears in my eyes, "Why do good girls act this way?" I wanted to understand why such sweet girls who love God would still act in an immodest way. And God spoke tenderly to my heart and shared with me that "girls are great at imitating what they see." Isn't that so true? All of us girls are always watching what others are doing, saying, or wearing. I remember imitating my mom when I was a little girl, pretending to be drinking coffee in a child's plastic teacup and using a crayon as my pretend cigarette, because my mom smoked cigarettes. I wanted to be just like her so I watched my mom intently, and then mimicked what she did.

Do you remember that little old song you may have sang, possibly in Sunday school, "Be Careful, Little Eyes, What You See?" Do you know that song? Well, compared to what some people might see, dirty dancing may not be all that bad. Yet, just like that song says, we truly need to be so very careful with what we allow to pass by our eyes. Otherwise, we will fail too, and end up imitating or duplicating what we have just watched.

Chaste becomes Chase

A friend of mine shared this with me: "When we take the 'T' out of the word 'chaste,' the new word becomes chase.'" And that's exactly what happens: when girls stop dressing chaste, then they become someone whom guys want to chase. That "T" in the word "chaste" is shaped like a cross. So, dressing chaste is a reminder to us that chaste is how God wants you and me to dress.

And remember, God only tells us "no" for our protection. He wants to protect us from huge heartaches ... Truly God knows what is best for us.

Watch Your Baby-Steps

An attraction to a guy, wanting to get closer to a guy, is something that God created within you; those thoughts and feelings are all normal. And every boyfriend relationship you will ever have will all start basically out in the same way. It starts usually with a look, to where you see each other and find each other cute or attractive. Then one of you will smile at the other; that will lead to casual talking, then possibly to holding each other's hands. Before long you might find that giving a hug to each other comes quite easily and often. A kiss is likely to follow from lots of hugs, and if you are not careful, from there it will lead to caressing and touching each other, and then most likely to the touching of personal body areas ... Girls, please be so very careful. These actions I just mentioned are all baby steps leading to sex. And you can find yourself in compromising positions so fast, because our attractions to people lead to real emotions or feelings for that person, and then our hormones kick in with real intense passions, to where we can be so easily tempted to go all the way (have sex) with a guy that we feel we are falling in love with. Please be wise, honest, and so very careful. Do not be alone with a guy—be wise.

Sex the Way God Created; it is Not Dirty

Please listen to me when I say sex is not dirty, and it's not evil. God is the creator of sex, and those desires and passions to have sex all come from God. He is the One who created all those hormones in us girls and in guys too. He made us all that way for us to be attracted to each other ... He did this so we would want to fall in love, get married, and have a family of our own one day. Sex is not a dirty thing at all, no matter what you have heard—it's a wonderful and beautiful gift! But God only allows for sex to be a wonderful and beautiful gift within a marriage union, between a husband and wife. Sex is God's gift to married couples. Within a marriage there is no shame that comes from sex; it's a beautiful blessing that has God's approval and encouragement.

Sex outside of marriage is plain and simply put, sin. Before marriage it's wrong to satisfy your desires and passions for sex with a guy. The Bible is very clear in this area:

> **"Honor marriage, and guard the sacredness of sexual intimacy beween wife and husband. God draws a firm line against casual and illicit sex."**
> ~Hebrews 13:4 MSG

I want you to know the truth about sex, because one day, some of your friends might tell you something different than what I am telling you. Your friend might tell you that she got real, close to a guy and it was exciting. And they will want you to do the same. (I had friends try to talk me into doing the same things with my boyfriend that they were doing with their boyfriends.)

Listen to me, please: you are not missing out on what they are doing, they are missing out on what you are doing. By your obeying what God tells you to do, you will one day reap the blessings of obedience. And those friends who are being pretentious, and ambitious, and not chaste, they will end up with broken hearts time and time again. Because sex outside of marriage brings deep emptiness and shame. And that's the sad truth.

Take a Stand Now

I once heard of a young guy bragging to all his friends, "We did it!" That is what this guy called sex with a girl: "did it!" Not "we made love and I love her so much!" This young girl lost her virginity and all he can say is, "Yeah, man, we did it!" How very, very sad ...

There are such blessings that come to those who stay pure, and wait for marriage to have sex. Your body is a gift to give to your husband one day, and it's the prettiest, most desirable gift you can give to your husband. Treasure the gift of your virginity; you can't put a price tag on the value your virginity holds. Don't let our culture allow you to think your virginity is nothing. On the contrary, it's **Something Very, Very Wonderful and Special!** I want you to take a stand now and decide now that you are going to remain pure until the day you get married. Because if you don't decide now, and take a stand now, one day you will find yourself in a situation, maybe not too far away, where you will want to compromise your values in staying pure. Maybe think about having your parents get you a purity ring; place that ring on your ring finger of your left hand, the same finger where one day you will have your wedding ring go. And as you look at that ring it will become a visible sign to you, and to the guys in your life along with your friends, that you want to wait for sex until you are married. You are deciding to honor God in obedience. That ring may truly save you from future heartaches ...

It's not too late

Precious girl, if after reading about sex, your virginity, and being chaste your heart becomes sad and guilt ridden because possibly you have already had sex with someone, please know it's never too late to start all over. And what I mean by that is, you can confess to God right now that you are sorry for having sex before you got married. And I promise God will forgive you. The Bible says that God can wipe out our sins and make them as white as snow, as if they have never even happened before (see Isaiah 1:18). In a sense, today you can become a born-again virgin, today you can begin to live the way God wants you to live. This decision may mean you need to break up with your boyfriend, or it may mean that you might need to make some changes with the friends you hang out with. Always remember it's way easier to pull someone down than it is to pull someone up. That is why it may mean in obeying God; you will need to hang out with different friends. You need to hang out with people who want to lift you up and not pull you down. Please confess to God today if you have fallen short by having sex before marriage. God will be faithful to comfort your heart and most of all offer you forgiveness.

Baring my soul:

I want to share with you a very real time in my life that I'm not proud of. In fact, I'm ashamed of it … I was in the eighth grade, 13 years old, and remember that guy Scott that I wrote about, the guy who got the many kisses? Well there is something that happened with him and that not too many people know about. You see, I was crazy in love with this guy at the time. And all I wanted to do was be with him. When I was with him I felt really special. He was cool and cute, strong, great at sports and popular. And to think that he liked me was simply amazing! He was the Bomb! So I thought … We had been dating for about two months; dating back then meant he'd come over to my house after dinner and homework, and we'd sit on my front porch and we'd talk about everything. And then we'd start making out. Kissing a lot, caressing and touching each other's personal parts … (I told you I'm not proud of this.) I honestly feel truly sad as I even share this with you… One day my friend who lived just around the block from me (and by the way she was dating Scott's best friend) told me that this coming Friday night her parents were going to be gone for several hours and wanted to know if I wanted to come over and hang out at her house. She said, "Let's invite the guys over too …" The anticipation for Friday night made my emotions go crazy! I was a bit frightened, thrilled, felt grown up, and it also made me feel very nauseous thinking all about how Friday night might go. I remember walking out the door that Friday night lying to my parents that yes, Teri's parents would be home, as I went to her house. Strike one. Right? ☹ As I walked over to Teri's house I looked good, smelled good, my hair was perfect, shiny lip gloss was on, and I had fresh sweet breath. I was ready to take Scott's breath away! I anticipated watching a movie with all of them and eating popcorn together. I also figured we'd be kissing a lot; I just wasn't prepared for how much further the night would go … Ugh. After watching one 30-minute show all together and eating popcorn, my friend Teri suggests to me, "Why don't you and Scott go upstairs into my bedroom while the two of us stay alone in the living room." With embarrassment and fear I said, "Alright." It was so awkward; I was afraid if I said no to going upstairs, I'd lose my time with Scott, and I wanted to spend time with him more than anything in the world. I also knew my friend was dropping a hint for us to leave her and her boyfriend alone, so we walked upstairs to her room. The only place to sit in her room was on her bed—ugh again. Luckily, she had a TV and we turned that on and watched some game show; I don't even remember what it was called. And then, you probably guessed it, Scott and I started kissing big-time, and before I knew it half of my clothes were off too. I was scared, so scared, and yet honestly my brain was thinking if I say no to Scott, he will break up with me. So, I started praying, "God, get me out of this, my thoughts are not making sense to me and I don't want to go all the way with Scott and have sex with him and get pregnant." All I could think of was the shame of getting pregnant, what heartache it would bring to my dad. And not to mention the total embarrassment it would bring to me. "Oh God," I cried, "help me!" God's help came to me as I finally got the strength to say to Scott, "I can't go any further." I remember putting my clothes all back on in record time, looking at him and saying good-bye to him, and then running down the stairs out the front door of Teri's house and running all the way home. I don't even remember seeing Teri in the living room. I never once stopped to look back ... I ran like my life depended on it, because at that time it did ... It wasn't long after that Scott and I broke up. He suggested to me that we could always do "other things" besides "going all the way," but I wasn't falling for that or having any part in or of it either. Girls, I share this very real story with the hope of saving some of you from not going down the road I came close to going down. I wish I could share the same thing happened to my friend Teri, but it didn't. About three months later she and her family moved to another city. I never saw Teri again, and rumor was out that she was pregnant ... My heart still hurts for her. Why couldn't I have been stronger to help her too???

Worldly Sex:

Now on the other hand, sex the way our culture portrays it is a dirty thing ... The world flaunts sexual images to us everywhere (magazines, movies, TV shows, billboards, books, commercials, video games, online, stores, and on our phones). Everywhere we go the world throws sex in our faces. I remember when my oldest son started college there was an ad stapled onto a public bulletin board that read, *I will pose nude for money.* That is not what this mom wanted to see! How sad for that young girl to be so desperate for money and to think not so highly of her body, or to know how valuable she and her body are. She was acting as if her body was just a Styrofoam cup. That mentality breaks my heart. Girls, remember how valuable you are! Like a treasured china teacup. Jesus died for you, and to Him you are His treasure.

Sometimes the music we listen to is bad:

Also, watch the songs you memorize and allow to get stuck into your heads. My son loves to play Guitar Hero. Do some of you like to play that too? There's a song that is kind of fun and upbeat, it's by a band named ZZ Top, called "Tush." The lyrics to that song got stuck in my head one day, and then I realized what I was singing: "I ain't asking for much, Lord, take me downtown I'm just looking for some tush." Now if we take those words of the song seriously, what the singer is asking for from God goes against God's very nature. He is not going to answer a prayer that will help you sin against Him. Looking for some "tush" is the singer's way of saying, "God, I need You to provide for me some sex right now. Just a little fornication, that's all." Now do you see how crazy that request is? And yet it's a very popular song with a great beat that gets stuck in our heads. That is why I say be very careful what music you listen to, because music has a way of influencing us in the wrong direction. Movies too! Please be careful of the movies and shows you allow yourselves to watch. There is a huge fan club for the *Twilight* movies. And honestly, I totally understand what attracts girls to the series: it's romantic, has good-looking guys in it, and offers a daring adventure. But girls, look at what you are viewing; are you really excited to see vampires fall in love? Now before those movies came out, if any of you were asked what you think of vampires most of you would say they are evil, scary, and always in horror movies. So now, *Twilight* the movie comes out, and the allure is amazingly captivating to us girls. And of course, it is—they have good-looking guys acting like vampires and werewolves. And a beautiful girl falls in love with one, and that draws our hearts to thinking this isn't so bad, because it's a love story. Right? Wrong! It's the trickery of the devil who is controlling this world. Some of you overlook the evil that is on the big screen while you get caught up in the romance of falling in love. But there is nothing godly or pure about that movie. And now some of you are hooked to see each new sequel that comes out. How many of you have ever asked Jesus if it's okay for you to watch the *Twilight* movies? Gulp, Gulp ... It's so important that you guard your hearts, minds, and bodies. When we watch movies that warp the truths of God, we take steps of compromise that lead to more compromises that eventually lead you and me to sin. Or at the very least they clog our ears from what Jesus would whisper into them.

> **"And now, dear brothers and sisters, one final thing. Fix your thoughts on what is true, and honorable, and right, and pure, and lovely, and admirable. Think about things that are excellent and worthy of praise."**
> ~Philippians 4:8 NLT

What a valuable scripture to put to the test in everything we hear or see or do. When we try to justify all the wrong things we do, we only end up fooling ourselves. It's for our own good to obey God's Word and His ways. And if you want to find a way to really get back at this dictating world and Satan himself, fall deeply in love with God ...

Beauty:

Beauty inspires and it invites, and it should draw us to God and not to the devil. As girls, we longingly ache to be told we are beautiful. Right? I know I do ... The truth is every single one of you girls is beautiful! You truly are! God made you a girl and a woman on purpose. And you are very beautiful. Every girl, and every woman in this whole wide world, has beauty to show. You have it because you bear the image of God; you were made in His likeness. And our God is so very beautiful that our eyes can't even look upon Him, because His glory is so bright, our eyes would burn if we saw Him.

The beauty you have was no accident; your beauty was given to you on the day you were created, when God formed you in your mama's womb (see Psalm 139).

I know each girl reading this book longs to be loved, treasured, and told she's beautiful. Believe me, sweetheart, you are! God, who created you, loves and adores you, and He says to you, "You are BEAUTIFUL!" (And He even says that about your dorky side. LOL. ☺) He sees you, He knows you, and He treasures you. And He tells you of His great love He has for you so you will grow to be strong, confident, beautiful, and chaste women. Women who have **Hidden Elegance** ...

I want to leave you as I close this chapter with this verse:

> **He replied, "The Father alone has the authority to set those dates and times, and they are not for you to know." ~Acts 1:7 NLT**

Trust Jesus with everything in your life, and take to heart that some things like "why doesn't that boy like you?" or "why do I like that guy so much?" or "who will I marry???"

are not for you to know right now ...

Don't choose the frogs out there; wait for your Prince Charming. He is worth waiting for ...

Prayer:

Oh, God, help us to have a heart for You, while we live in a real world that wants to destroy our hearts. Give us the strength to be like the China Teacups as we strive to live for You each day. Thank You for how much You love us. We love You too. Amen.

CHAPTER 4

Fear: Inside and Out

What makes you afraid? Think about that for a minute. If we are honest, all of us have some type of fear we deal with. Our answers may vary on the fears we do have, but I think we all have them. One of my real fears is that I don't like being alone in the dark. This fear started when I was young girl; I think my brother and sisters scared me too much hiding behind doors or under beds just to jump out at me and cause me to scream—all in fun of course. Yet, it left me with an eeriness of the dark, and ever since then I like the lights on and I prefer the daylight. I can remember turning the lights off in my bedroom to go to sleep, and suddenly fear would grip me as I imagined all kinds of monsters were around me and they were trying to attack me. So, when it was nighttime and as I walked down the hallway to my room, I'd turn on every light there was leading up to my room. When I finally shut my bedroom light off to go to sleep, I kept a little night-light on so I could see better—for my safety of course! My parents were always telling me, "Don't forget to shut the lights off," because everywhere I walked there was a light on. Darkness still really creeps me out. And things always seem different in the dark, don't they? I think most of us are all afraid a little bit of darkness, and maybe it's because our eyes don't see things as well in the dark, or maybe it's because at nighttime that's when all the critters come out. You know like the rats and roaches, spiders, and monsters ... Ugh!

What about scary music—does the sound of it freak you out or not? You know what I'm talking about, like what they play at haunted houses. Even the haunted house at Disneyland plays scary music! Whether scary music gets to you or not, it sends a message to your brain that something is just not right, and to be on the alert. Right? My husband has this shock game where four people hold a trigger handle in their hands; you push a button to start the game, and as you start the game it plays scary music, and then when the music stops each player needs to squeeze their trigger as fast as they can, and the last person to squeeze their trigger gets a shock from the handle. My husband loves this game! I, however, don't like that game because I'm afraid of getting shocked, and the scary music just intensifies it all! ☹

What else makes you feel afraid? How about spiders? Ewe! I hate spiders! I mean, I really, really hate them! Or I am really, really afraid of them—however you want to say it. LOL. Before I became a mom, I would never kill a spider, I would always get someone else to kill them for me. But then, when I had my first baby, I didn't want a spider to bite him, so, if one came around us and no one else was home, I'd have to get brave enough to kill it. It still gives me the willies to have to smash a spider, and then what do you do with the tissue you just smashed the spider with? I always flush them down the toilet rather than throw them in the trash, I guess because I'm afraid somehow the spider lived through my smashing and will crawl back out of the trash can ... At least by flushing them they are gone for good! Right? How do you feel about spiders??? I heard this really cool story one time where a pastor had been sharing the Gospel in Africa. It turned out that his message wasn't going over too well with the village people, and the next thing he knew he had 50 men chasing after him intending to hurt him. This pastor began to run up a rocky hill, and as he did, he saw a small crevice of a hole to hide in. He knew it was only a matter of a few minutes before the men would find him. But just after he crawled into the crevice, a spider came out and started spinning a web over the opening of the crevice. And several minutes later when the men came near looking for him, they looked at the hole of the crevice and there was no tear in the web, so they figured this pastor was not inside, and they left. Can you believe that spider story? Can you even imagine what that pastor was thinking as he sees this spider cover the hole, he's in? I think compared to getting found by the villagers, having to defend himself from a spider is a piece of cake. I love hearing stories like these, because it shows me how Big our God is—that he can even use the things we are afraid of for our benefit and even for our protection. That spider wasn't just chance when it came out to form its web: that was God telling that spider to move!

So Many Fears

Arachnophobia is the fear of spiders, and Acrophobia is the fear of heights, Agoraphobia is the fear of being in crowds, and Claustrophobia is the fear of tight places (like in an elevator or in a closed-up room). I once had a cat that had claustrophobia; she hated being in one of those pet boxes that you carry your animal in when taking them to the veterinarian. She would rip and tear at the box until she was out. This one time, we were getting ready to move from our house to a different house. So, while the movers were in our home moving all our furniture, we put this cat into one of the empty bedrooms with her litterbox and food and water and closed the door so she couldn't run away while the movers were about. And she would cry and try to rip at the door and the carpet. Gosh, she didn't want to be in a closed area of any type, not even a big bedroom. That cat was known for ripping holes in the screens of our windows and tearing up our screen doors to the house to try and let herself outside. She was afraid Big-time of not being able to leave a certain place.

There are all kinds of phobias that people live with. Psychologists say there are around 183 phobias right now. And did you know the very word "phobia" means fears devoid of logic or senselessness? That means people are being afraid for **no** good reason! I think some of our fears might be irrational, but not all of them are. Right? Because I know, I really am afraid of spiders …

How about horror movies—do they scare you? I don't like scary movies at all! I remember when I was little, my brother and sisters would watch this show called *The Twilight Zone*. Have any of you ever seen that show? They're kind of like a 30-minute mystery and suspense story with a twist at the end of them. They're created in an imaginary weird way, causing you to think, what if this happened to me? There was this one story about this little girl who got a doll delivered to her house. And this doll turned out it could walk and talk. It could do more than just talk; it could think and reason. It ended up being a robot that was sent by a bad guy, who had designed this doll to kill this young girl's uncle whom she had lived with. That show really freaked me out! Because I had a lot of dolls, and at night when it was dark in my room, I would imagine my dolls were all coming alive and their eyes were opening and moving. How could I go to sleep after watching that? It freaked me out big-time! Ugh!

Have you ever seen the movie *The Wizard of Oz*? If you have seen it, remember that mean lady who would ride the bike with the basket on it, and she always threatened Dorothy that she would take her little dog Toto away? And remember how she also became the Wicked Witch of the West? Well, when I was young I had a friend who lived on my block, and her mom looked just like the mean lady or the wicked witch in *The Wizard of Oz*. She even rode a bike like the one in the movie, with a basket on it. And I had a little dog too, and I would imagine her stealing my little dog away from me ... She frightened me so much! There are parts of that movie that I love and other parts that I don't like much at all ... Movies sometimes have a way of drawing us in, and then we wish we would have never ever seen what we just saw. Right? Do you ever wish you wouldn't have watched a certain show or movie because what you just watched has freaked you out in a bad way??? Yeah, me too ... ☹

When I was a teenager, I saw a terrible movie called *The Exorcist*. It was awful—I mean really, really horrible! And the only reason I saw that movie was because everyone else was seeing it. And I felt like I wouldn't be cool or fit in if I didn't see it. (I was following the popular crowd.) So, I broke down and went to the movies to see it, and I'm not kidding: through half of the movie my eyes were closed and my hands were over my ears. It was about a young girl who became demon possessed, ugh ... Looking back, I wish I had never given in to the crowd and watched that movie ... It totally FREAKED me out! And what I saw in that movie stuck in my mind for years. Sometimes even scary movies can become addictive. To me, it seems like anything the devil has his hands in becomes addictive ...

Are any of you afraid to ride roller coasters? I'm both afraid of them and love them all at the same time. Kind of like a love-hate thing. When the ride first starts, I'm so afraid, but by the time the ride is over I can't wait to get right back on and ride it again. Does that sound familiar? Why do you think we are that way? I think it's an adrenaline rush or something. One time, my family and I went to Knott's Berry Farm, and it was one of those perfect days where there weren't any crowds. The first roller-coaster ride we went to was called The Silver Bullet. Have any of you ever been on that ride? We had a blast on it! And after going on a few other rides in the park, we headed back to The Silver Bullet. There were no lines to wait to go on that ride, so as soon as the ride ended, we'd get right back into the line and ride the Silver Bullet again. After riding it for the fifth time in a row I was feeling dizzy, and I knew I'd had enough of The Silver Bullet—my brain couldn't handle any more movement or jerkiness. That ride started out as so much fun, then became addictive, and then ended up making me sick. I learned the hard way that something fun can turn out to be not so much fun when you overdo it.

Feeding our Imaginations

Sometimes, our imaginations get the best of us. Whatever we feed into our hearts and minds by movies, video games, books, music, magazines, and the internet—things that are not good for us to be watching, viewing, or listening to—the scarier our dreams can be. You see, our imaginations feed on what we take in, and if we will guard our hearts and minds from frightful things, then it is less likely we will have bad dreams. Yay for no nightmares! Sometimes if we've seen a lot of bad things, it can come back to haunt us, because it can be so hard to get those images out of our minds. I also believe the devil doesn't want you to forget the scary things you saw, because he wants us to be frozen in fear. The devil has all kinds of methods he uses in trying to create fear in us. But, girls, it's our choice to choose whether we will buy into his fear tactics or not. You get the choice to watch a scary movie or not, choose wisely what you watch ... You see, the Lord loves to see us full of peace so we are effective and useful. But, the devil loves the opposite of what God loves; he desires to see us sidetracked and fearful so we are not useful in helping others.

We can also be afraid of natural disasters, like earthquakes or tornados. I live in an area that is known for having a lot of earthquakes.

And even though I've lived through many earthquakes, they still frighten me every time one occurs. They are not fun! I'm sure if some of you live in tornado areas, they aren't any fun either. These are natural disasters, things that are out of our control when they happen, and I believe it's totally normal to have fear when they happen. In fact, that fear can cause us to take wise action in seeking shelter for our safety when they occur.

Are any of you afraid of sharks? After seeing the movie *Jaws*, I became very fearful of sharks. Every time I go into the ocean, I'm always wondering what's in the water with me ...

Maybe your fears are snakes, or alligators, airplanes, elevators; or maybe your fear is to have to stand up in front of class and do an oral report. Whatever your fears may be, God will ALWAYS prove stronger than our worst fears. Please don't ever be afraid to ask Jesus for help with anything—He truly lives to help us (see Hebrews 7:25).

Baring my soul:

I feel like for me I've wrestled with a lot of fear in different ways throughout my life. I'm very sensitive to scary movies and being in dark places like I've already shared with you. I like it when the lights are on or the sun is out. But, honestly, one of the most frightening times for me was learning to adjust to a stepmom and a stepbrother. My dad remarried when I was 13 years old, and the weird thing was, he married my mom's younger sister. So, my aunt became my stepmom and my cousin became my stepbrother. Weird, right? My life back then felt like a soap opera in many ways. Adjusting to my stepmom was difficult for me, not to mention a stepbrother. I had someone new to be the boss of me, and my stepmom did boss me around and I did not like it one bit! Not quite Cinderella, but I felt like it at times. I had to share my bathroom with my cousin/

stepbrother, and he was gross! I mean really gross! For the first time in my own home I didn't feel safe. And I didn't like being in my home. I felt like I had been invaded, surrounded by strangers and having no privacy. I was miserable. You see, my mom's sister had lived in another state, and one summer my dad went to this state to see his sisters and other family there and ended up falling in love with my mom's younger sister. Her name was Grace, and she had been a widow for ten years before my dad married her. And because she had lived so far away, I had really never known her, and she was WAY different than how my mom was, even though they were sisters ... I remember being very depressed and hanging out mostly in my bedroom, where I could shut the door and pretend nothing was different. Although everything changed the minute I stepped out of my room. I cried a lot, and I was afraid to tell my dad that he and his plans were the problem. My stepmom stuck up for her son more than for me, even when he was in the wrong. And when I would try to talk to my dad he wouldn't let me just talk with just him alone, he insisted that Grace be included in every conversation. So now I felt like I had lost my dad on top of losing my mom ... Oh yeah, see the end of this book on how I lost my mom ... Losing my mom was the scariest of all; this new family was the second scariest. A sense of hate began to grow inside of me over my stepmom and stepbrother. I felt like I tried, like I really tried, to get along with them, but I believed they thought I was spoiled rotten and they even told me so. So, I isolated myself after school in my room; in there I felt somewhat normal, somewhat safe ... In time, things did change, but it took a long time, years for the hate to go away in my heart and for love to enter in. Fear is a very real thing, and my fear was rooted from great sorrow. For those of you girls who may be dealing with stepparents too, please hang in there—time has a way of changing things. Know, sweet friend, that you are not alone because Jesus is always with you. Draw close to your friends, or another family member or even one of your friends' moms—someone that you trust—so they can love and encourage you in this fearful time of your life. I ended up talking to my sister Diane; she is 12 years older than me and she truly became my second mom that God knew I would need ... What I know now that I didn't know then was that God was holding my heart when it hung so low and He was capturing every tear that I shed, and there were many, many tears, tons of tears ... I pray if you are struggling right now with a stepparent, or maybe over something with your own parents, that you will feel a little more hopeful after reading my story. Grace and I did end up having a very sweet and loving relationship after a while. So please hang in there, and talk to Jesus about what hurts you the most ...

Living with Fear

Did you know that you operate or function at your poorest when you are fearful? When you live with fear, it destroys how you function normally. It robs you of your hopes, the dreams you have, and the drive in you to keep going on. As I'm writing this chapter right now, the Lord has led me to think of how some of you who are reading this book have seen some really hard things in life that have happened to you that are so tragic and scary. Maybe you've lived through natural disasters like a tornado, or an earthquake, or a fire, or maybe a car accident, or watching someone close to you battle drugs or alcohol, witnessing abuse, or seeing a loved one die.

These types of fears occur in real life, and they are not choices we choose but things that have happened in our lives out of our control. My heart grieves for you, if that is where you are at ... Oh, precious girl, how I wish I could take that pain and fear away from you ... And how I wish I could reach out through this book and give you the biggest bear hug ever. Please know this: everything that you are dealing with is no surprise to God. He is right beside you, and He will carry you if He needs to. Our wonderful God longs for you to reach out and talk to Him so He can love on you and embrace you completely.

God longs to see you smile again. I know this because I have lived through much pain and sorrow. And Jesus was the One who walked with me through all the heaviness and fears I had. Look up right now if you need a hug, or to hear sweet words of hope. Ask Jesus for these acts of love that you crave; there is no one who truly knows you better and all that you are going through than Him. I don't say this in a light manner in any way, but only from truth and real-life experience, that Jesus is the only One who can clear your mind and take that fear away ... Please also look for someone close to you that you trust, and share your heart with them. Be as honest as you possibly can about your fears. We all need love and support from others in our lives, so don't be afraid to ask for help.

And know this: it is a lie from the devil who whispers in your ear that life is too hard, and that to end your life would be the best thing you could do. That is a HUGE LIE! Thought up in the deepest, darkest part of hell. The devil is the father of lies.

> **"The thief's purpose is to steal and kill and destroy.**
> **My purpose is to give them a rich and satisfying life."**
> ~John 10:10 NLT

And his mission is to rob, steal, and destroy from you and I, all day long. He wants to rob you of joy, hope, peace, and love. He wants to steal away your dreams. And he wants to destroy any plans God has for your future. Yes, God has wonderful plans for your life, ones that will bless you more than you could ever imagine, and that's the truth!

> **"For I know the plans I have for you," says the Lord.**
> **"They are plans for good and not for disaster, to**
> **give you a future and a hope."** ~Jeremiah 29:11 NLT

Jesus is for you! He is on your side. And He wants to restore back to you all that the world has scared out of you. Please, please choose to let Jesus be that big in your life.

"His wonderful thoughts towards you are more than the sands on the sea shore." ~Psalms 139:17–18 NLT

Think about all the sand at the beach, each little grain, and God says He thinks of you more than all those grains of sand. That's more thoughts than I can imagine ... Girls, every time you hear whispers in your ears, that life is not worth living—resist it! Say back in your own mind, "No, that is not true! My life is worth living, for Jesus tells me so! I call those evil whispers "Horn-Flakes," because they are dark thoughts meant to hurt us, and steal our joy away. Horn-Flakes makes sense to me because it reminds me of when I eat a bowl of cornflakes. While I'm eating cornflakes, they are so crunchy that I can't hear what other people are saying. Or if I'm watching TV, I need to turn the volume up while eating a bowl of cornflakes because of the crunching that is going on in my mouth. That's exactly what the devil does to us when he attacks our minds and whispers creepy thoughts at us. We get worried, stressed, fearful, depressed; there is a loud buzz going on in our minds just like the crunchy cornflakes. Thus, the nickname of why I call his attacks Horn-Flakes.

So, keep saying "this is not true" in your heads and before you know it, you will have resisted the devil enough times that he will flee from you, along with those dark thoughts he whispered at you.

"So humble yourselves before God. Resist the devil, and he will flee from you." ~James 4:7 NLT

And one day that fear you had, though it was real and hard to live with, will go away. Not forgotten, but not controlling you anymore. God will show you in time how faithful He is, and turn all that you've gone through into good. God has a special way of doing this ... And in His beautiful plan, He will use you to help others who are struggling with the very same things you have gone through. Imagine that? That through the scariest times in your life, you will one day be able to help another person as they go through the same things you've gone through. I think that's super cool! We all need people to share our own real-life stories with. As we find similarities with others, it helps us to connect with them, and brings comfort and a source of healing. We all desire to have people love on us, and walk with us, when we are struggling. That's what gives us hope! We need each other ...

God Wants to Take Away Your Fears

God wants to take away the fears you have that hold you back.

> **"Such love has no fear, because perfect love expels all fear."**
> ~1 John 4:18 NLT

Fear is a very powerful influence in our lives. It can take over our thoughts, and cause us to not want to go anywhere or do anything. The devil wants to see us frozen in fear, but God wants us to be brave and step out in faith into the things he has for us.

> **"For God has not given us a spirit of fear and timidity, but of power, love, and self-discipline."** ~2 Timothy 1:7 NLT

My pastor says, "There is no darkness Jesus is afraid of." I find that so comforting to hear; may that comfort your heart as well. No matter what you are struggling with or going through, Jesus is not afraid of it ...

Did you know that the way a psychiatrist would treat someone with certain phobias is by having them face their very fear, like riding on that elevator 50 times in a row, or having them touch or hold a spider—Ugh! They might also take someone who is afraid of heights to the very top of a high-rise building. Psychiatrists have their patients face their fears head on so they will learn that their worst fear did not happen. In the same way, there may be times God will allow you to go through a difficult time for you to grow from it, and not be afraid of it anymore. For instance, like talking to new people, smashing a spider, walking in the dark, or giving an oral report. Remember Moses in our bibles? He had to pick up a snake before it turned back into a rod. Or David killed a bear and a lion when he was out looking after his sheep. And through those victories it gave him the courage to even kill Goliath. (see 1 Samuel 17)

Don't Dabble Here

Unfortunately, when we are afraid sometimes, we look to other things rather than to God for guidance and help. Girls, do not ever dabble into astrology. Dabble means to take part in or consider it. Do you even know what astrology is? It's when people look at their horoscope, or go to a palm reader, or even a fortune-teller. You are not defined as a Libra or a Gemini like in astrology, you are God's daughter, and that makes you unique and so loved and so full of wonder that only God gets to say who you are. God is the one who will design your life, not some weird hocus-pocus mystic person or some dark video or board game like a Ouija board; they're all bad and they all have the devil's fingerprints on them. These are not just bad, they're truly evil. That's why I say don't even touch them or dabble into them. Some people think, I would never go to a fortune-teller, but then they look up their horoscope every day and live by what it says. All these things fall under the sin of divination.

Listen to what God says about divination:

> **"And do not let your people practice fortune-telling, or use sorcery, or interpret omens, or engage in witchcraft, or cast spells, or function as mediums or psychics, or call forth the spirits of the dead. Anyone who does these things is detestable to the Lord. It is because the other nations have done these detestable things that the Lord your God will drive them out ahead of you."** ~Deuteronomy 18:10–12 NLT

God hates these practices because they have power from the devil. Therefore, God tells us to have nothing to do with any of them. Anything having to do with divination needs to be avoided!!! Why do we even get so excited about our fortune in a fortune cookie at a Chinese restaurant? I think it's because deep down we want to know our futures. But God says, "Trust Me, and I will take care of your future," and that should be enough for us. I'm so guilty of liking to read my fortune in those cookies too.

The truth is our world can be a very dark and scary place to live in. You can turn on the news every day and read of natural disasters, terrorists, wars, murders, rapes, and kidnappings. Kidnappings make me think to share with you that it's very important for you to watch the places you go. You need to be very wise and make good decisions that the places you enter are safe. I'm talking about staying close enough to others where someone can always hear you if you had to cry out for help. And hang out with those whose character is good. If you don't know a person well, then do not be alone only with them. And I know you may not like to hear this, but always tell someone where you are going; your parents are your first choice to tell.

I also know you are struggling with fears of inferiority too—Big-time! Right? I can honestly tell you that your fear of not measuring up to others is just not the truth even though it feels like it is. You are the girl God wants you to be and whom He made you to be. There is no one in this whole wide world that is just like you, so why do you even compare yourself to anyone else? We are all different and uniquely made. We need to stop comparing ourselves to others and start living life the way God sees us and wants us to be. I believe when God made you, He said, "Yes!"

Your bodies are also going through huge changes right now ...

Most of you have hormones raging and even peaking to new heights in your bodies. Mentally and physically, you are changing and becoming women. This time in your life can be kind of scary too.

True Story

I remember being in the fifth grade and starting my period at school. Remember that story I shared with you in the friendship chapter, about starting your period and if you had anyone you could trust? Well, that was me. It was recess time at school, and I was on the monkey bars and a friend asked what was on my pants. I lied and said I had a cut. I doubt she believed me, but I was too afraid to tell her the truth. The truth was I had started my period, and I really didn't understand at the time all the changes that my body was going through ... I also remember pushing down on my breasts, not wanting them to grow. (My breasts started to grow when I was in the fourth grade, and I just wasn't mentally ready for it.) And my mom was a very private person who didn't share openly with me about all the changes that were taking place in my body. She didn't share with me about my period early enough; I found out the hard way by living through it. Girls, the more wisdom your mom can share with you the better. Receive it, take it all in—your moms have a lot of valuable information to share with you, and you have so much to learn from them. Yes, I know talks about body changes can be somewhat embarrassing, but those talks with your mom and by your mom are so important. And trust me, it's not easy being on the mom end and having to talk about certain things either. Your mom is your best resource for truth—remember that! It is a beautiful thing to grow and mature in becoming a woman. (Now I do all I can to push my boobs back up! LOL!)

With all the hormones raging in your bodies, you are also going through huge emotional changes too. In your minds or in your heads is where you struggle with worry and anxiety. And it's there in our minds where the devil once again goes into overtime attacking us with negative thoughts. Do you know what the term "Trinity" in our Christian faith means? It means that we believe in God the Father, God the Son, and in God the Holy Spirit. We call our God a triune God because He is three deities in one God. God designed our bodies to be three in one also. We are body, soul, and spirit. Our body is our flesh and bones; it's how we move and function. Our soul is our minds; it's who we are and how we think, our personality. And our spirit is our inner hearts; it is how we can talk and pray and communicate with God. In Luke 21:19 it says,

"In your patience possess your souls." NKJV

Girls, that means it's our patience that controls our minds. How many of you would say you are patient? I honestly don't see very many patient people these days. It seems like we are always in a hurry. Yet, God tells us it's the very secret to ruling our minds. The next time you are in a hurry, remember what I just told you. When you put God at the center of your minds by praying and talking to Him, or reading your Bibles and allowing a certain scripture to captivate your thoughts, then, you won't be so easily tripped up by the devil's games that he attempts to play on you and me in our minds. You see, the devil can't invade our hearts if Jesus lives there, so he, being clever, goes to our minds and attacks them with thoughts like these: You're not as smart as her, her bedroom is cooler than yours, everyone is looking at your zit, she doesn't like me, I look fat, I'm too tall, too short, I'm not smart, I can't run fast, I wish I could sing, why don't any boys like me? On and on the devil will keep playing these mind games with us. Sound familiar? (Horn-Flakes.) Everyone struggles with thoughts like these. The devil is so clever and mean; he brings up the one thing that personally bothers us the most. And then, guess what happens? We get all worked up over it and we lose our patience with everything and with every-one. We stress over something that most of the time is not even true. Girls, you are the only ones who can control your minds. You are you, and your mind is you. If you don't want to allow all those games to go on in your mind, then you need to take control of ev-ery thought. With patience ruling in your minds, then peace comes in, and that peace comes from focusing on Jesus ...

There are about 365 scriptures on fear in our Bibles. That's enough for us to read one for every day of the year. I only shared a few with you in this chapter, but you can find hundreds more on your own. I think they are all there for us because God wants you to know that you can trust Him and he doesn't want you to live in fear. And listen to this: nothing ever surprises God—He literally knows everything! That means He knows how much havoc the devil will try to cause in each of our lives. The bible says the devil is a roaring lion, and that his very nature is to cause you to be terrified.

"Stay alert! Watch out for your great enemy, the devil. He prowls around like a roaring lion, looking for someone to devour."
~I Peter 5:8 NLT

If a real lion broke out of the zoo, wouldn't you'd be afraid? I certainly would! God wants you to know that you don't have to fall prey to the devil. In a very real sense, you could say Jesus has already hunted the devil down with an eternal silver bullet. Jesus conquered and defeated the devil on the cross. Yes, and amen!

Girls, when you are looking in the right direction, you won't take the wrong turn. Reread what I just wrote. And then read it again.

I once saw this nature show where there was a baby bear that was walking in the forest when he came upon a big mountain lion. The baby bear then stood up on his hind legs and stretched his front legs as high in the air as he could and gave the biggest roar he could muster up. The camera lens slowly widened to let you see the background of what was behind the baby bear. And there was his mama standing on her hind legs looking like a huge monster. That mountain lion took one look at Mama Bear and ran away as fast as he could. All the while Baby Bear had a proud look on his face. ☺ In the same way, Jesus has got our backs too.

I heard this story that I thought was worth sharing with you: A long time ago a certain Persian king sent to Judah, the prince of Jerusalem, the largest diamond known in existence. And upon receiving this gift, Judah sent back to the Persian king a copy of the book of Deuteronomy with an accompanying note that read: "What you have sent to me requires guards to protect it. But what I have sent to you will guard and protect you." I so love that story! Does it make sense to you? Let me try to break it down for you: If someone gave you a big beautiful diamond, and upon receiving it you are told that this diamond is the rarest in all the world and that it's worth a crazy amount of money, you might think, Wow! What should I do with it? And how will I keep it safe from people who will want to steal it from you? Or you could be given a bible, and as you open your bible and begin reading it, something stands out to you that you just read and it makes your heart feel happy. So, the next day you reach for your bible again hoping to read something else to comfort you. And to your surprise you read something again in your bible and you love it! Then days, weeks, months go by and you realize that reading your bible every day has caused you to be less fearful, has brought you peace, and has helped you feel more loved and secure. In fact, it brings you comfort more than anything else does. Your bible ends up being your go-to when you are worried about something. Well, in much the same way as in that story, God's Word truly becomes our treasure, it ends up guarding and protecting us with a sense of peace and joy. God has an amazing way of bringing the words we read to life to us personally. I can't even tell you how many times I've read a verse in my bible that came alive in my heart and captured all that I was thinking and feeling so perfectly! So, don't put off reading your bible today; I pray one day it will become a treasure to you too!

In Closing

When you run to the world when you are afraid, you will never find assurance. Only when you run to Jesus do you find safety, security, and sweet peace. Say no to your fears that cause you so many tears, by saying yes to Jesus! Then you will put muscle to your faith and sense that Jesus is ever so near.

Prayer:

Dear Jesus,

Help us to trust you with all the giants that come our way, and help us to feel your mighty arms around us so we will know we are in the safest place possible. Amen.

CHAPTER 5

Balance is the Key

My hope for you from this last chapter is that you will find some true nuggets of wisdom to take with you for the rest of your lives. Finding balance in life is hard for most people, but for a woman it's sometimes the hardest thing to accomplish. If you don't believe me just ask your mom or any woman you know, and they will tell you it's hard to stay balanced. And I mean really hard for some of us.

Sounds cliché but seek God First

The first thing you must learn to do is to seek God first in your day before anything else. Or at least do your best to do so, even if you only have a few minutes' talk to Jesus and ask Him for His help and favor over your day. Or pick just one scripture to read and say a simple prayer before reading that verse; maybe something like this:

Dear Jesus, help me to understand what you want me to learn from Your Word today.

The reason I share that it's important to seek God first is because He asks us to do so; listen to what Jesus says:

"Seek the kingdom of God above all else, and live righteously, and he will give you everything you need." ~Matthew 6:33 NLT

What that means is as you start your day off with Jesus, He will be faithful to take care of the rest of your day.

Cute Story

There is a cute story about a grandpa who lost his pocket watch somewhere in his house. So, he told all his grandchildren that the first one to find his watch got a crisp twenty-dollar bill. You can imagine the kids and how excited they must have been looking for their grandpa's lost pocket watch in hopes of earning twenty dollars, but sadly no one found his watch that day. Early the next day when their grandpa woke up and came down the stairs, there was little Billy, his grandson, standing with a smile on his face. "Here's your watch, Grandpa," Billy said. The grandpa was so surprised and thankful, and asked Billy how he found it. Billy said, "It was easy, Grandpa, I just got up early while the house was quiet and listened for the ticking." What a smart little guy.

And the same is true in your home when you seek God early in the morning: it's usually a quieter place to be in, and that makes it easier for you to hear God speaking to you because there are fewer distractions. I know getting up early probably doesn't sound good to you right now, but one day that might change. It's totally up to you what time you want to read your Bible; the main thing is that you do make time in your day to be with the Lord.

Jesus said,

"people do not live by bread alone, but by every word that comes from the mouth of God" ~Matthew 4:4 NLT

Your faith grows stronger as you take in the nutrients and spiritual calories of the Word of God. Jesus wants us to include Him in our daily habits. You remember to eat breakfast or at least lunch and dinner, so then start remembering to make it a routine to read your Bible too. And something you might not think about or realize is, whenever you are talking to Jesus you are actually praying to him, so whatever you do, keep on talking to him. ☺

The 3 "G" Sins

I'm convinced every girl, every woman, will wrestle with one of these three "G" sins throughout her lifetime; for some it may be a battle with two of them or even all three. And I have found that these "G" sins can and will keep us from spending time with God.

The First is Gluttony

Gluttony is the first "G" sin we will talk about. When someone battles with gluttony, it means that they eat too much food, which oftentimes causes their bodies to become overweight or obese. Simply said, they eat more food than their body really needs. Sometimes this "G" sin carries over into more than just food; it could be that they are obsessed with clothes, and buying clothes in excess makes them feel comforted or happy, much in the same way as food can comfort us. Or maybe they want more shoes than they can wear, or they want every new type of makeup or perfume that comes out. Our personalities come into play with those things we may obsess over, but basically, it's the action a person might take with having too much of anything.

The Second is Gossip

Gossip is the second "G" sin. I don't think I need to define what gossip is. We all have been a victim of gossip, or worse we've been the ones doing the gossiping. It's a sin that is everywhere. And its means you are saying something or hearing someone else say something that you have no business in hearing it or passing it on to others. Gossip truly is a dangerous weapon. We need to watch it, ladies. Seriously! It's so easy to get trapped by it. Listen to what a wise man inspired by God wrote:

> **"Too much talk leads to sin. Be sensible and keep your mouth shut."**
> ~Proverbs 10:19 NLT

I don't need to add anything more to that; it was perfectly said.

The Third is Glory

Glory is the third "G" sin. And this relates to someone who is always looking or wanting to be the center of attention. I'm sure you've met girls like this, who without fail must be in the spotlight or be the focal point of whatever is going on. Sometimes it's normal to desire some attention, but if you need it constantly it can become an obsession, and that's not good. These types of people have a selfish mentality and are jealous of anyone else getting all the attention.

Do you see yourself with any of these "G" sins? I sure do. Sometimes, I think I'm guilty of all three of them. ☹ I'll share later with you which one of these is the greatest struggle for me ...

Healthy Eating: What does that look like?

The second thing I'd like to talk with you about in this pursuit for balance is basic nutrition. I am finding through God's wisdom that the foods that are good for my mind are also the ones that are good for my body as well. Go figure. Right? Foods such as meats, breads, dairy products, fruits, and veggies are what make our whole-body function at its best. That's a no-brainer. Right? Healthy foods make our bodies healthy. Truly, you think clearer when you eat healthier food. In much the same way as gasoline is fuel for our cars, food is fuel for our bodies. Do any of you know what happens to a car's engine if you put diesel gas in a car that is not a diesel-fueled engine? The engine blows up! In the same way if you only feed your body with junk food it might not blow up, but it will break down. Meaning when you and I make poor choices with the food we eat (always eating junk food), then we will tend to be tired a lot and less likely to want to do any activities inside or outside, and we tend to catch every cold virus going around. I'm sure some of you might have all felt tired after eating a bunch of junk food. I know I sure have! We honestly don't think as sharply when our diet has no healthy foods in it. Some of us crave salty foods like chips, crackers, nuts, or popcorn. And others of us crave sweets like candy, cookies, cake, or ice cream. Whether we have a salty tooth or a sweet tooth, our junk food intake needs to be eaten in moderation and not constantly. Did you know that the more junk food we eat, the less likely healthy foods will even taste good to us? It's true, take, for instance, an apple or any other type of fruit; it's sweet to our taste buds, unless we've shied away from fruit and have only been eating cakes, or cookies, or candy—then fruit tends to taste sour compared to a sugary-filled dessert. The truth is when we eat the food God made naturally for us, our bodies are healthier and we feel better too. God made food for our enjoyment, and we must eat food to survive, so I'm not saying you can't ever eat a sweet dessert again, or a bowl of popcorn; I'm just saying try your best to think more in a balanced way, and take the time to think what kind of fuel you are putting into your bodies.

True Story:

I remember this one time; my whole family went to a really nice restaurant for my dad's birthday. We were having brunch at one of those all-you-can-eat restaurants, and honestly, they had everything you could imagine to eat, including so many amazing desserts! There was a girl who was having brunch with us, who was a relative of my stepmom's family. She was probably about 13 years of age, and she was really pretty. Anyhow, after eating a plate of food and a small plate of desserts, she went back to the buffet and got some vegetables and a tiny bit of salad. I asked her if what was on her plate sounded good to her to eat (the salad and vegetables) with all the other choices there were to choose from. She said to me, no, but she felt like she needed to put something healthy into her body instead of all the rich fancy foods she had been eating. This young girl knew her body needed good-fuel foods and not just junk-fuel foods. Oh, how we need to learn her wisdom!

Pray before you eat

Jesus modeled for us to pray for our food.

"Give us today the food we need." ~Matthew 6:11 NLT

"So whether you eat or drink, or whatever you do, do it all for the glory of God."
~1 Corinthians 10:31 NLT

Praying and thanking God for your food before you eat it is a good habit to get into. Every time you eat something, even if it's just a snack, thank God for it. And it doesn't need to be a long prayer, just a simple prayer like,

"Thank you, Jesus, for this food."

Pay attention to what your body needs

Girls, if you don't eat, you won't have the energy you need for your day. Remember food is our body's fuel, so when you neglect eating, your body stops working, the same way a car does with no gas in its tank. The car's engine may start up on an empty tank, but it only has fumes to keep it going, and soon it will stop running altogether. The same goes for all of us: we need fuel in our bodies to start our days and to finish them. Think about your typical day at school. You are there for around eight hours, which is a long time, and you know you are going to get hungry while in school. So, it's important to plan to take a lunch to school, or maybe just bring some healthy snacks to eat to give you the energy you'll need to get through your whole day. Even a peanut butter and jelly sandwich can be filling and healthy, and it's easy to make and we all usually have those staples in our kitchens. Or if you are buying your lunch at school, remind yourself that you need to give your body some good fuel foods too, so choose a piece of fruit with whatever else you are buying or a side salad or some carrots. Look down on your lunch selection and find something healthy to add to it. Sometimes a piece of fruit can be way more filling in your stomach than a bag of chips—truly it can.

Try to make eating fun and enjoyable; be daring and try different healthy things to eat. Have you ever tried jicama before? It's a root vegetable and the outside of it looks ugly and gross, because it grows under the soil or in the dirt, but when you cut away its rough exterior skin the inside is white and rather sweet and juicy, and it's a vegetable! Give jicama a try, and I bet you will like it. ☺

Eat with your family and eat with your friends and allow your taste buds to be open to trying different foods; otherwise you'll never know what you may be missing out on. Jesus ate with his friends, and did you know we will even be eating in heaven? It's true, check out (Revelation 19:6–9): there's going to be a BIG feast!

Warning

Be careful when you are all alone because that's when most people tend to eat emotionally. When we eat emotionally, we feed our minds and not our bellies. This is usually caused by stress, boredom, anger, fear, sadness, or any emotion; even being super happy can cause us to eat. Emotional eaters tend to overeat because their minds never get full, so when their bodies start giving them signs of fullness, they ignore those signs and keep eating.

Drink water

It's also important to drink water. Water in its purest form is best. That means not vitamin water, carbonated waters, or flavored waters; while those are good for something different to drink occasionally, they should not be your only water intake. Water truly helps our bodies stay balanced. In fact, water is the most major necessity for all living things. It is a great choice to drink water instead of a soda, juice, ice tea, or coffee. Water cleanses our bodies, blesses our skin, hair, nails, and all our internal organs. We take water for granted, but it truly is a gift from God to be able to drink it. Try even putting a slice of lemon, lime, orange, or cucumber in your water to spruce up the flavor.

Baring my soul:

If I could be really honest with you, the "G" sin I struggle with is gluttony; it's my core sin. And if you remember what I said before, that means overeating excessively. I'm really embarrassed over this and deep down I hate even admitting it to you. I truly would rather keep it hidden and not let anyone know what I struggle with. But I believe part of the way God wants to save me from this sin and heal and restore me is by exposing it to the light, confessing it before Jesus and to you ...

> **"But you desire honesty from the womb, teaching me wisdom even there."** ~Psalms 51:6 NLT

Sometimes I think it's the worst sin to have to deal with, because food is everywhere and it's a necessity for all of us to survive. When you think about getting together with friends and family it usually revolves around food, and it's fun to entertain with food along with making food with people—or at least I really enjoy it. And if you are anything like me, you might like to bake with your mom at Christmastime, or help prepare a birthday cake for someone special, or maybe you love helping to prepare the Thanksgiving meal with your family. Those times are so much fun and such a treat to enjoy with our families and friends. And although we all tend to overindulge with all the special foods around the holidays, those occasions are not the only times where I struggle with overeating. I struggle on plain normal days, where I will binge on food, and just eat way too much! For instance, if I have a bag of Cheetos, I can't eat just a handful of Cheetos and then stop. No, I want to eat the whole bag, and well, honestly, I can eat a whole bag in one sitting! The truth is I've stopped counting how many bags of Cheetos I've eaten in my lifetime. Yeah, that's me—"oink, oink!" I told you this is the real me, and I'm not talking the snack-size bag, I mean the big one that has several servings in it. The condemnation after eating that whole bag of Cheetos is that I feel like a big fat pig. And I also feel like I truly hurt my body: my stomach hurts and I feel sluggish and tired, like I just want to lie down or go to sleep. The sad part is I hate how I feel after eating the entire bag of Cheetos, but while eating them it sure felt good and I enjoyed every bite. It's the after-effects that get me. It's the guilt that I'm left with that robs me of joy. Even though it was fun or pleasurable at the time, it becomes depressing afterward. The fact is there is always some type of pleasure in sin; otherwise we wouldn't be attracted to it. I'm drawn to salty foods, and even though I know I shouldn't eat them, I still occasionally do, and rather than making a good choice by eating just a small amount, I eat way too many or far too much! I guess I can say that salty junk foods are my comfort foods, my go-to foods when I'm upset about something ... Ugh! I crave salty foods like chips, popcorn, or Cheetos; I can pass on sweet foods most of the time. For instance, if there was a plate of chocolate brownies or a bowl of chips and salsa set out on a table, I would choose the chips and salsa every time. As far back as I can remember I've struggled with food ... ☹

True Story #2:

I can remember when I was 14 years old going on a vacation with my girlfriend, we went to a lake where I was going to try waterskiing for the first time. My friend and I went down to this little general store at the resort where we were staying and we both bought a large bag of nacho cheese Doritos, a candy bar, and a diet Coke. Why the diet Coke I don't know, with all the calories in the chips and in the candy bar? I guess somehow it made our minds feel better about ourselves. Anyhow, I remember telling my friend before we bought our snacks that I could eat the whole bag of chips on my own and that we should buy two bags. That was a big deal to admit that to her, as it was my first time ever telling anyone about my overeating habits. And honestly, I couldn't believe it when my friend said she could eat a whole bag of Doritos too; somehow her words comforted and confirmed to me that it was okay to eat all those chips. Her "G" sin was gluttony too. So, we each bought our own bag of Doritos. And back at our campsite in the trailer that we were sleeping in, we stayed up half the night talking as we ate away at our snacks. I wish I could say that was the last time I ever ate that much food, but it wasn't ... I'm learning with the help of Jesus to control my cravings and not to give in to my temptations, or give in to my emotions, but there are days where I still find myself falling short. And always after I've binged on some food, I always feel so guilty, and I regret it sooo bad that I gave in to the temptation, not to mention my stomach hurts because I fed it WAY too much food! (*Note to self: eating a whole bag of Hot Cheetos or Nacho Cheese Doritos stains your fingers and it's hard to hide the evidence. LOL!) Remember when I shared with you to be careful of eating all by yourself, or when you are all alone? Well, it's because when I overeat, or binge, or pig out, it's usually when I'm all by myself, so I just wanted to caution you to be careful too. I'm wondering if some of you might even admit that's when you struggle too? No one is around and I'm usually thinking to myself, if I eat something now, no one will know, it will be my own little secret ... And I think the devil always tempts me during those times when I'm by myself because that's when I am at my weakest. You know the Bible tells us that Satan is like a roaring lion seeking whom he can devour.

> **"Stay alert! Watch out for your great enemy, the devil. He prowls around like a roaring lion, looking for someone to devour."**
> ~1 Peter 5:8 NLT

When I watch those nature shows of wildlife on TV, whenever a lion chases down an animal to kill and eat, it's always the baby of the herd or the injured animal or the older, slower, weaker one.

Lions go for the easy prey ... And I think when I'm all by myself without the help of my husband or family or friends around me, that's when the devil creeps in and pounces on me for the kill and starts bringing thoughts into my mind for me to be tempted to eat ... Ugh! Oh, and here's the last truth of confession about overeating: I never binge on healthy foods, like eating six bananas, or too much broccoli—no, it's always with junk food. Sigh ... It's best for me to not even buy those salty tempting foods to have around me in the house. There's an old saying that says, "Out of sight, out of mind." And that is so true, because when I know that there is junk food sitting right in my kitchen pantry or refrigerator, then my mind starts craving it, and I can't stop thinking about that certain food; you might say I start obsessing over it. And obsessing over anything is never a good thing. The truth is I know that Jesus loves me so much, and when I spend time with Him and read my Bible, I find Him to be the Greatest Source of Comfort to me. Hands down, the comfort I receive from God has no comparison to the comfort I get from food. Zilch! Nada! So why can't I just remember that every time I choose food for comfort instead of Jesus??? I hope somehow with me sharing this "G" sin with you, it challenges some of you girls to face your struggles too. All I can tell you is if you battle with overeating like I do, then be on guard when you are alone and all by yourself, for that's when you will most likely be tempted to overindulge with food. Every time you find yourself alone, that's the right time to invite Jesus in and ask him to help you with your cravings. We need to get to the point of understanding that God wants to bless our hearts way more than food ever will. And when we don't learn that truth, we can be sure that the devil will sneak up on us with a pounce—in for the kill—to tempt you and me with an enormous amount of unhealthy junk food to eat. We need to be on guard and ready to say "No" to our temptations. It's a hard thing to do, but it is possible ...

Eating Problems

Some people struggle with eating disorders. An eating disorder is when a person eats food in an abnormal way which causes harm to their bodies. I'm just going to touch on these subjects, but again, it's a balance thing, and usually those who have eating disorders are listening to their minds (emotional eaters) instead of their stomachs, like my problem in overeating.

Anorexia

A person with anorexia suffers with an unrealistic view of their body and always sees themselves as fat. They look at themselves in a mirror and have a distorted and untruthful view of what is reflected in that mirror. Although everyone else would see them as thin or skinny, they see fat where there is none. Kind of like looking at yourself in one of those funny mirrors at a carnival or at a fair, where the mirrors make you look short and fat, but it's just a warped mirror designed to make you look that way so you will laugh. Those who suffer with anorexia see themselves this way in every normal mirror. They live with great fear of becoming fat. Usually for those who suffer with anorexia, their body weight is roughly around 15% below normal body weight. Which means if a girl's normal weight is 100 pounds, one who suffers with anorexia would weigh around 80 to 85 pounds or even less.

Symptoms of Anorexia

Discontent with their body's appearance, irregular menstrual periods, struggles with anxiety (worry, fear, or nervousness), body weakness and tiredness (no energy), brittle hair and dry skin (making their skin more prone to cuts and bruises); they can have shortness of breath in walking or exercise, and they won't want to eat in public. Girls, if you know a friend who you think might have anorexia, please tell your mom, or an adult you trust. And if after reading these symptoms you think that you might be struggling with this problem yourself, then it's truly time to tell someone; there is help for you, or for the one you know and care about.

Bulimia

A person who struggles with bulimia usually is obsessed with food, goes to food for comfort, eats an abnormally huge amount of food, and then secretively gets rid of the food they've just eaten. Most commonly they rid the body of food by forcing themselves to vomit. There have been times in my own life after I have eaten way too much food that I wished I could self-vomit, but I just couldn't do it. I think it's because when it comes to vomiting it feels so bad or painful to me, that I can't bring myself to do it on purpose. Vomiting sucks! I don't think the person who struggles with bulimia would say that they like to vomit either—no one does. But this person can reason to themselves that it's less painful to vomit than live with the mental pain of gaining weight. Sometimes, a person who struggles with bulimia may exercise in excess to burn the calories they've eaten, or they may find alternative ways to rid the food, through laxatives, diet pills, or they may not eat for two or three days after a binge-eating time.

Symptoms of Bulimia

Discontent with body shape and weight, lives in fear of gaining weight, feels as though they can't control their eating behaviors, eats to the point of pain or discomfort, irregular menstrual periods, teeth erosion and cavities, ulcers, heartburn, swollenness and soreness in their glands in their throat.

Other Problems

Other abuses done to the body are cuttings; this is when a person cuts themselves on purpose, inflicting pain and causing scarring to their skin. Self-imposed burning: this acts in the same way as cutting, but rather than cutting themselves they burn themselves with a match or a candle or other fiery object. Pulling their hair out is another, and also, an abnormal number of piercings to their skin. All these bodily afflictions numb the emotional pain where they are truly hurting (in their hearts) and give the self-abuser a false sense of control. Oh, girls, I can't stress enough how much a person who struggles with these disorders needs loving help. Their self-inflicted pain is masking the real issue that is going on in their broken hearts. ☹

"Don't you realize that your body is the temple of the Holy Spirit, who lives in you and was given to you by God? You do not belong to yourself, for God bought you with a high price. So, you must honor God with your body."
~I Corinthians 6:19–20 NLT

Oftentimes, those who struggle with food problems or those causing bodily injury to themselves suffer with a much deeper pain going on in their hearts. God always looks at the heart of the matter. Remember what I wrote in the beginning of this book? *I realize what happens in a young girl's life now is life lasting in her heart.* It's honestly in our hearts where God wants to bring healing to everyone who struggles with eating problems, or abuse of their bodies, or just with any type of hurt we are keeping hidden. When we abuse our bodies in any way, we may hide it for a short amount of time, and do our best to keep it a secret, but after a while the truth usually comes out. Even when I overeat, the truth of what I'm doing is evident and noticeable by the weight I've gained. My hope and prayer is for those who may be struggling with any of these harmful issues will feel the loving eyes of Jesus looking at them, and that they will know that they are HIS beautiful work of art, His masterpiece! Sweetly listen to that: you and I are God's masterpieces …

> **"For we are God's masterpiece. He has created us anew in Christ Jesus, so we can do the good things he planned for us long ago."**
> ~Ephesians 2:10 NLT

He has created us brand new; we get to start over with second chances and third chances and fourth and fifth! God's love for us is so amazing! And He will keep helping us every time we mess up. My sweet friend, may you embrace the love and open arms Jesus extends to you all the time and at any time …

Exercise

Exercise is any activity that trains and improves the body or mind. The purpose of exercise is to develop and maintain physical fitness. Plain and simply put, by exercising you are promoting life to your body. I suggest you make exercise fun! What is an activity you like to do? Pick that one and do it. Exercise promotes better sleep, more muscle mass, and creates a faster metabolism which burns more calories, strengthens our bones, gives health to our heart and all our major organs, and makes our hair and skin healthier too. Truly exercise does a body good! *Walking in the mall counts as exercise! ☺

Baring my soul again:

I remember when I was in junior high school, I always wished I could run well, or maybe I should say I wished I could run fast in PE. But, no matter how hard I tried, running never came easy for me. I remember I would start running fast, but would soon lose momentum because I couldn't breathe or catch my breath. And before long, I'd quit running altogether. Defeat would take over in my mind as I saw others passing me on the track, and that made me want to give up even more. I had good intentions but lacked wisdom and understanding in how to run in the right way. So, I gave up on my desire to run. Until ... one day, when I was in my forties (yes, you heard me right—forties), I joined a women's boot camp where running was a big part of this program. And I must admit when I first started running in boot camp, I was terrible at it, and once again, it made me feel terrible ... It was hard to breathe when I would run (like when I was younger), and all my past thoughts came back in my mind and I started to doubt my ability, and thought to myself I might as well just give up now ... Running was so tiring; it made me sweaty and I hated it! UGH! I even had a personal issue to where if I ran too much or too fast, my bladder would end up leaking—it was so embarrassing! I would literally dribble out pee in my pants. I would wear mini pads to prevent my shorts from getting wet. It was so embarrassing. But you know what happened? After a while, something changed in me: running started to grow on me, and I got kind of good at it. On top of that my muscles in my upper legs and in my calves got stronger and pretty defined, which made me happy and proud of myself. My bladder muscles even got stronger and I was no longer having those leaking issues. Thank You, Jesus! I found out that I could breathe better and go further in my running attempts. And then guess what? I found myself missing it if I didn't run for a while. My boot-camp instructor had taught me to run, then forced me to run, and it ended up growing on me. Now I run on my own; it's my choice with no one telling me to do it. So, truly, anyone can learn to run—I'm living proof of that. And honestly, whether you are a beginner runner or a veteran runner, running is always considered hard work. You see, God created our bodies to go into protection-mode when we feel pain, or when we can't breathe. Our minds will look for a way to stop the pain we are feeling, and it's usually by telling us to quit the exercise that we are doing. The secret to running or any type of physical exercise is figuring out that it's your mind that you need to strengthen the most, not your legs or your lungs. You see, when you first start to run there will be a battle going on that you must face. Everything in you, your whole body, wants you to stop running; even your mind will tell you to quit. You will feel overwhelmingly tired, you won't be able to breathe, and you'll probably get a cramp on one of your sides, or your foot will start aching or something like that; it always happens—something hurts when a person first sets out to run. The thing you need to do is tell yourself I'm going to do this, I can do this, and I will not die (LOL). Then plan your running routine with a goal in mind on how far you will run. It must be a realistic goal, like don't plan for a mile the first time you start to run, because a mile may not be an attainable goal for a beginner. Maybe aim more for like an eighth of a mile, which is a half lap around the track. Once you run that far for a few days or a week, then slightly increase the distance of your next goal in running. A week later set a new goal, and before you know it you will be up to a half a mile, which is two laps around a track, and then soon at a full mile. I used to run with junior high girls when it was their mile day in PE in school. And as I ran the track with them, I'd encourage the girls by saying, "You can do it, just slow down your pace, don't go too fast, just breathe," and lastly, "You're doing great!" I was their personal cheerleader. I'd tell them that the hardest muscle they will exercise while running is their minds. If they could just keep telling themselves that they could do it, they would eventually be able to run the full mile every time. Yes, it's hard, but it is definitely doable! And the girls always felt so good after their accomplishment! I think those girls thought to themselves, *if a mom in her forties can run a mile, then we can do it too.* Plus, I would reward them with popsicles on occasions.

Remember the exercise you are doing right now; you may not like it—in fact you may hate it—but one day it could end up growing on you, to where you find yourself truly liking it. Girls, part of staying in balance starts with exercise now while you are younger, and then by making it a habit for the rest of your lives.

No Excuses for Exercise

Even when you are on your periods, that time of month, your menstrual cycle, don't neglect to exercise. I know you will need to take precautions (maybe wear extra pads), but don't shy away from PE or even going out for a walk. By exercising during your time of month, it will even help with mood swings, food cravings, cramps, and headaches. Exercise truly helps us stay balanced.

Rest

Lastly, rest means sleep. It's so important for you to get enough sleep. Listen to this: If you are average weight and height, this is what your body will go through in a 24-hour period of time. Your heart will beat 103,689 times, your blood will travel 168 million miles as your heart pumps approximately 4 ounces of blood per beat, you will breathe 23,040 times, inhaling 438 cubic feet of air, your stomach will take in 3 ½ pounds of food and 2.9 quarts of liquid, you will have lost $7/8$ of a pound of waste (that means #2), you will move 750 muscles and exercise 7 million brain cells, and a girl will speak 7,000 words." That's all in one day. Whew! No wonder we get tired by the end of the day! ☺

Listen to how Webster defines sleep in the dictionary: "it's the natural periodic suspension of consciousness during which the powers of the body are restored." Sleep, in short, is our time to regain strength and energy. All our bodies get restored while we sleep. It's kind of like how we charge our phones every night so we can use them the next day. Sleeping charges our bodies. I know at your age you want to stay up late at night, but honestly, if you are a preteen or teenager you need more sleep than ever. Your bodies are going through rapid growth cycles and your hormones are changing at alarming rates; sleep truly is your friend—always remember that! I know you don't need anyone to tell you what time to go to bed on a school night, I just want to be a voice in your ear that reminds you why you need your sleep. Just call sleep for what it is: it's our Beauty Sleep—truly it is!

Listen to This

Balance. Balance. Balance ...

If you don't eat enough food your body gets tired, so you sleep more and feel lazy. But what your body really needs is food, not more sleep!

If you don't sleep enough, your body craves more food to give it a false sense of energy. But what our body really needs is sleep, not food!

And if you don't exercise it will diminish your appetite, and the food you do eat won't digest properly, and you won't sleep as well. It's all a balance thing.

Remember This

What God gives us to do each day is doable.

In Closing

Picture an orange in your hand; better yet if you have an orange at home, go get it and then continue reading.

An orange – It's simple and beautiful. It is something meant to be eaten and enjoyed. It is healthy and tastes good. And it's in sections to be shared ... It's in perfect BALANCE ... And it's <u>no</u> wonder, for only God can make fruit. ☺

Prayer:

Dear God,

Help me to remember that I am beautiful just the way you made me. Please help me to make good choices each day with the food I eat, with exercise, and getting enough sleep. Help me where I am weak and make me stronger.

Thank You, Jesus, I love You ...

"You saw me before I was born. Every day of my life was recorded in your book. Every moment was laid out before a single day had passed." ~Psalms 139:16 NLT

My Story:

Once upon a time, a baby was conceived by a husband and wife who loved each other very much. And as this mother carried her unborn child, she became very ill during her seventh month of pregnancy. She was taken to the hospital and underwent emergency surgery because this mother's intestines had become entangled. This was a delicate surgery as her baby was growing in her womb. After several hours of surgery both mama and her fetus were resting safely, and three days later they got to go home from the hospital …

A little girl was born on June 21, 1963, to Mrs. Barbara Philippon and to her husband Mr. John Philippon. She was the fourth child born to her parents—not planned by them, but planned by God; they named her Mary Ann. She had two sisters, one 12 years older and the other 11 years older than her, along with a brother who was 8 years old when she was born. She grew up in a happy and loving family.

It's me ☺

I've been told, as a baby, I loved having my back patted; you know, kind of how you burp a baby? And my favorite time for this patting was as I was falling asleep. As a young baby my crib was in my brother's room, so that meant my brother had the chore of patting my back when I stirred after my mom put me to bed. And at first my brother didn't mind patting my back (so I've been told), but after some time of patting my back my brother would pick up his dirty tennis shoe and put it on my back. And I thought the whole time it was his hand and slept like a baby ...

I shared my sleeping arrangements with each of my siblings—first with my brother David with my crib in his room, and then off to each of my two sisters' rooms.

As I grew out of the crib, I shared a room with my oldest sister Diane, and we slept together in a full-size bed. I remember being maybe around three years old asking her questions like, "Why do we wake up with sand sleepies in our eyes?" And, "Who is the Sandman anyways?" (I was told the Sandman is the one who while we slept would put those sleepies in our eyes.) I guess I couldn't understand the concept of how eye boogers got into my eyes every morning. I also remember asking my sister if she could please cover me up with the blankets. I know, crazy sounding, right? Somehow, I couldn't figure out how to roll and adjust my position in bed trying to fall asleep and pull up my own blankets all at the same time. Go figure—sounds a bit spoiled to me, but I needed someone to tuck my blankets in. Then, because of keeping my sister Diane up all night with my many questions and asking her to cover me up in the middle of the night, she kicked me out of her room and I was off to my second sister's room; her name is Linda. In her room, I had my own bed; we had bunk beds and I was on the top bunk. Linda would listen to the radio every night to fall asleep, so I would ask her questions that came from the songs we were listening to.

Questions like, "Why do raindrops keep falling on his head? Why doesn't the guy just get an umbrella?" Or, "Why did the lights go out in Georgia?" "Why? "Why? Why?" I always asked a bunch of questions, my poor sister. It's kind of funny as a mom now; my boys tell me I still ask a lot of questions too ... LOL.

I remember when I was five years old, my sister Diane was going to take me to the drive-in movies. And I had never been there before so I was super excited! We were going to eat homemade popcorn, drink Kool-Aid; I'd get to wear my pajamas and slippers, bring a blanket and pillow and be all cuddled up without ever getting out of the car. And then my sister said she would buy me a candy too from the snack bar! WhooHoo! Could life get any better for a five-year-old??? The movie we were going to see was a Disney movie, and on top of that a cartoon, she told me, and that I was going to love it! I couldn't wait to see it! There I was eating popcorn, laid back in my pajamas all comfy and cozy, watching a movie that was so fun! But then, something happened midway through the movie that got me so upset. And I got really sad and, in a way, fearful; it was something so devastating I couldn't even imagine it happening in real life. You see, this really cute deer, well, his mom got killed in the movie ... Yes, you guessed it, the Disney movie I saw was *Bambi*. And it didn't matter how happily the movie ended, because in my heart I couldn't get past the thought of when Bambi lost his mom. At five years old, I told my sister that this was a horrible movie, and I was so mad at her that she even took me to see that movie. A little bossy attitude, don't you think?

... Little did I know that seven years later, my own life would become a Bambi story ...

My Bambi Story

At the age of 12 years old, I'm the only child still left in my parents' home. My sister Diane is living on her own in a nice apartment, driving a nice car, and has a nice job as a nurse at a huge hospital. My other sister Linda is married, living in an apartment with her husband working as a dental assistant, and my brother David is in the United States Navy, married and stationed in Hawaii. I had just finished my second week of junior high in the seventh grade. Life was new and exciting, starting with a new school, new teachers, new friends, and new boys to check out! I found myself trying to fit in everywhere; I just wasn't fitting in at my house ... You see, for the last couple of years I saw my mom changing a lot. She was drinking alcohol a lot ... At first, it was just a beer here and there or a glass of wine, but before long every day it was a drink at 4 pm, then another at 5 with my dad, and another at 6 pm with dinner. I can remember watching my mom take a beer with her lunch instead of a soda with me. I also remember my mom buying a big box of wine every week, and by the end of that week the box would be empty ... Although I didn't understand it at the time, I know now my mom was becoming an alcoholic. Do you know what an alcoholic is? (An alcoholic is a person who drinks alcohol in an excessive amount, to the point where their body becomes dependent on the alcohol, and if they stopped drinking the alcohol their body would go through withdrawal symptoms.) I watched my mom slowly changing before my eyes, and I hated it! There were a lot of things that embarrassed me about my mom, but this was becoming the biggest thing to be embarrassed over ... I hated seeing my mom get drunk! She acted funny then, maybe weird, and I just knew she wasn't herself when she drank and I hated it!

It was a Saturday morning around 9:30. I had just crawled out of bed eating breakfast, when my parents walked into the house; they had been out early to hit a local swap meet. I said hi to them, and

I could tell that something wasn't right with my mom. She didn't look like she felt good. My dad told her to sit down at the kitchen table while he got her a beer. The word "beer" irked me in a bad way, and I yelled out, "Gosh, Mom, it's breakfast time, you know—coffee, juice, milk, not a beer right now!" And my dad raised his voice to me and told me to be quiet and that he'd had enough of my mouthing off to my mom. He told me she didn't feel good, to where I blurted out, "Ya, Mom, and a beer is supposed to make you feel better???" I said it in a very disrespectful way. (In fact, I said way more than I should have ever said, but in my defense, I was mad, sad, hurt, and confused.) My dad yelled at me again, while my mom just stayed quiet and gave me a sad kind of mad look, so I was off to my bedroom slamming the door behind me. About 15 minutes later my sister Linda called on the house phone (no cell phones back then) to ask if I'd like to come over to her apartment and swim in the pool there. I was thrilled I got to swim in a built-in pool, plus get out of my house and away from my mom and dad, whom I was so mad at. Linda and her husband came and picked me up; we got in our bathing suits and were swimming in her pool for only about 20 minutes when her husband came to the pool and whispered something in Linda's ear. I didn't think anything of it until Linda said, "Come on, Mary Ann, we got to get out and dry off and go." "What? Why? We just got here???" She was getting harsh with her voice and I could tell by her tone she was very serious, to the point that I knew I needed to get out of the pool and go. She said to me with tears in her eyes, "Mary Ann, it's Mom, she's in the hospital and we have to go see her!" Now I couldn't even think straight. *What is going on?* I wondered to myself. I had just left my mom not too long ago; I knew she wasn't feeling good, but I thought it was just a cold or the flu coming on her ... So, what could it be? She's in the hospital??? We dried our bathing suits off fast and just put clothes over our wet swimsuits, and my brother-in-law drove us quickly to the hospital. My mind was in a blurry fog; I couldn't focus on reality. It was like someone else was living my life for me right then and there, just not me ... I watched my sister from the backseat wipe away tears. *What's going on?* I wondered. We arrived in the ER at the hospital and my sister Diane was there with my dad; I walked over to my dad and he said to me, "She didn't make it, your mom is gone." What??? Blur, blur—" What are you talking about, where is Mom?" I cried. And he told me how he had tried to drive as fast as he could to get her to the hospital, going through red lights and all, but it was too late ... My mom had died of a massive heart attack, and although the doctors had tried their best to save my mom and resuscitate her, they could not bring her back ... Blurriness again ..." Where is she? I want to see her!!! But they wouldn't let me see her ...

The reality that my mom wasn't coming back was more than I could bear. Back at home I could see her stuff everywhere: her clothes, her slippers, her jewelry, her coffee cup, her ashtrays (yes, my mom smoked cigarettes too), her towel, her perfume, her makeup, her wine, her beer. There was evidence of her all over the house, but she wasn't there ... People—friends of our family and others from our church and neighborhood—started bringing food over; we had so much food! Our neighbors would come and hug me and tell me they were so sorry for the loss of my mom. It was a week of this before her actual funeral. On the day she was to be buried, I remember a huge black limousine parked out in front of our house to drive my whole family to her funeral. Again, blur, blur—what is happening to me? "God," I cried, "I just want my mom back! Is this really happening, is this real?"

I remember after her funeral and getting back home, I went running into my bedroom, slammed the door behind me, and flopped on my bed, crying out to God for help. I felt numb; now what's going to happen to me? Why should I live anymore? What worth do I have? I'm a loser who fought with her mom and lost not only the fight but also the person? *Why? Why? Why?* is what I cried out to

God! My tears and my crying were uncontrollable. My heart never hurt so bad before. I felt like my heart had literally been ripped in two; it was even hard to catch my breath. Somehow, I was hoping this was all a nightmare and my mom would be back in my life again. I cried and cried, "God, please give me back my mom ... please." My sobbing was loud and I couldn't stop crying even if I wanted to. I kept saying, God, if you are real, I need to know, I need to know; help me, God, if you are real ... Tears, sobs, moans, and heart-wrenching pain throughout my whole body ... During this time of gut-wrenching sorrow, something happened supernaturally ... You might not even believe what I'm about to share with you ... But God met me. God made Himself real to me. You see, I grew up hearing the stories of all the miracles Jesus had done, and all that I had learned came crashing down in my mind, and I was crying out to God, saying, "God, if You are real, if You are really real I need to know? I need to know right now!" I was so scared and so full of pain and sorrow that I couldn't imagine how to live anymore without my mom. So, I cried out to God; no, I sobbed, panicking with streams of tears and snot pouring down my face as I desperately cried out to Him. And girls, in the privacy of my room, God supernaturally reached out to me. I was frantic and fearful and desperate, for I felt I had no one else to reach out to. Then God's presence filled my room; I could feel God, and He felt like warmth with thickness, almost like a fog but without the moisture of fog. And I'll never forget the words He spoke to my heart ... He said, "I'm here, My child, I'm here." His words were so perfect! Because I desperately wanted to be somebody's child. (I had my dad still, but my mom was my whole world even though I didn't treat her like she was.) And now somehow, I had become God's child? I cried out to Him, "God, help me, I need You, take my life because I can't go on any-more on my own ..." Girls, He brought such comfort to my heart that I can't even describe. He brought such peace to my broken heart. And most of all, through snot-filled tears, I could sense that He forgave me, as I told God I was so sorry for fighting with my mom and being mean to her ... He started to lightly lift the burden of my guilt that I would have to deal with for the rest of my life ...

"The Lord protects the simple hearted; when I was in great need, He saved me." ~Psalms 116:6 NLT

My life was different now! Somehow, I felt there was a purpose to it. I would counsel my friends not to argue with their parents, because some things just aren't worth arguing over ... Even though I was only 12 years of age, I felt like I was a lot older, like I'd matured almost overnight ...

Things about my mom

My mom was older than my friends' moms were, and I was embarrassed about that. My mom smoked cigarettes and drank alcohol, and I was embarrassed about that. My mom had a gap between her front top teeth, and that would embarrass me. My mom didn't wear the "in" style of clothes, yet she always looked clean and well taken care of, and I was embarrassed about that. My mom couldn't sing well in church, yet she would sing out loud and that would embarrass me. All these things and so much more would embarrass me about my mom. But girls, I would take all the embarrassing moments, all of them piled up together and more, just to have her back ...

Now that I'm grown, I understand the sensitivity I had when I was 12 much better. You are at the age of being so impressionable; everything matters greatly to you right now. It's not that you make too big of a deal over things, it's that for you right now things are a Big Deal! I totally get that. Totally get it! But girls, let me tell you one day you too will be an adult woman like me, and you'll find yourself thinking, I wonder what my mom would have done if she was going through this right now? All I have left are memories—memories of 12 short years that God has allowed me to remember. Yes, memories are a gift from God. Learn to appreciate your mom for who she is now, and don't dwell on how she embarrasses you. You know what? All those things that embarrassed me about my mom, wasn't her problem, it was mine ... My friends didn't really care; they thought my mom was nice and loving. It was me; it was pride on my part wanting everything to be perfect. But life isn't perfect, and no person is perfect either. Yes, my mom had a huge drinking problem; that probably contributed to her early death. But nothing I went through was a surprise to God. He knew everything that was going to happen. Could it be maybe God allowed for me to go through this very sad time in my life for a greater purpose? Like, to share my Bambi story with you?

Meeting Jesus

Just like in the movie *Bambi*, I had to look to my Great Heavenly Father to help me survive and find guidance, strength, and love. Losing my mom caused me to have to lean on Jesus. God in His amazing wisdom knew He would gain my mom in heaven and me as His daughter on earth. At the age of 12, I gained a relationship with Jesus for the first time in my life. My life went from chaotic to renewed in but a few moments of time, because Jesus made Himself known to me ... I would hate to relive the pain of losing my mom all over again, but, if by me sharing my story with you, and if only one girl asked Jesus to become real in her life, then all the pain that I went through in losing my mom would be worth it, and for God's glory! If you find you're asking yourself, "Is God really real?" I want to tell you, in a loud voice through this page, YES, GOD IS REAL!!! And if your heart is beating real fast right now, it could be because Jesus wants to come into your life, even right now at this moment. Please don't push those thoughts away—all of them are real that you are feeling and thinking about. It's Jesus wanting to come into your heart and life, and in a sense, you could say Jesus is knocking on the door to your heart because He wants to live with you and give your life new meaning and purpose. What are you waiting for? What's holding you back? Trust me, it will be the most important decision you will ever make—and the best one, I might add. All I know now is that Jesus lives inside me, bringing me life, love, purpose, and mostly hope. Hope of knowing that a great castle in heaven awaits me one day, with a God who wants to spend eternity with me loving me, and the hope of seeing my mom again ... God is my heavenly Father, my Parent and my Dad forever who will never ever leave me ...

Last Thoughts

Girls, I remember thinking that I was smarter than my mom (she doesn't know the math I know or the spelling I do) ... I thought my mom was such a nag (always telling me to do this and that). I was so quick to argue back and had to be right even when I was wrong. I remember feeling like she was so old-fashioned in her dress and the way she thought of things in life situations, but now I truly think she was cool, and I'm proud that she had such strong morals, and I love how giving she always was to her friends and to our neighbors. She had lots of friends, and everyone always loved coming to our home for the holiday parties like the Fourth of July and New Year's Eve.

But then reality hit, and she was no longer there for me. One day she is here and the next day she is gone. Unless you've ever lost someone so close to you like I did with my mom, it's so hard to even comprehend what I'm talking about. The pain and fear is huge! Little girls are not supposed to ever lose their moms, but sometimes it does happen, and it's so, so hard.

I couldn't do my own laundry like she could. I couldn't cook a meal for myself like she could. I couldn't even clean the whole house like she could. I couldn't drive myself to the mall to be with my friends, but she could. I couldn't give myself a hug like she could give me. And no one like my mom knew something was hurting me just by looking at me, but she knew …

We all have those prideful thoughts that we know more or think we are better than our moms, but the fact of the matter is we don't know more and we aren't any better. And it's not until you lose your mom that you understand this truth and concept completely. After my mom died, I would have given anything to hear her nag me once again, or make me breakfast perfectly again, or hear her sing a song out of tune in church again—or just to see her wear a dorky outfit again would be great! Or mostly, to feel her hug me just one more time … Oh how I miss her!

At the age of 12 my life changed radically. I remember sharing with my friends that arguing with your mom is just not worth it! So, you disagree and you could be right in your own opinion, but the fact is she's your mom and she's the only mom you have. So, try to see things through both her eyes and yours. Don't be stubborn, because no one in all this world is better at being your mom than she is. And no one in this entire world could ever replace her. And one day you're going to think back like I do, what would Mom have done?

In closing, sweet friend, would you do me a huge favor? Would you go right now and give your mom a hug and tell her that you love her? If I have made an impact on you through this book, in honor of what God is doing through this book, please go hug your mom and tell her that you love her. In heaven, I'll get to tell my mom that I love her again, and may I never stop hugging her …

My love, sweet friend,
Mary Ann
xoxo

"**And I am convinced that nothing can ever separate us from God's love. Neither death nor life, neither angels nor demons, neither our fears for today nor our worries about tomorrow—not even the powers of hell can separate us from God's love. No power in the sky above or in the earth below—indeed, nothing in all creation will ever be able to separate us from the love of God that is revealed in Christ Jesus our Lord.**" ~Romans 8:38–39 NLT

Amen …

*Please check out this song on YouTube: "All I Ever Have to Be" by Amy Grant. It's a go-to song, when I'm feeling a bit down.

CPSIA information can be obtained
at www.ICGtesting.com
Printed in the USA
FSHW010031141119

9 781977 215727